G000061282

ALL IN

ReganBooks
An Imprint of HarperCollins*Publishers*

ALL IN

POKER NIGHT LESSONS
FOR WINNING BIG AT YOUR CAREER

GEOFF GRABER
WITH MATTHEW ROBINSON

ALL IN. Copyright © 2005 by Geoff Graber. All rights reserved. Printed in the United States of America. No part of this book may be used or reproduced in any manner whatsoever without written permission except in the case of brief quotations embodied in critical articles and reviews. For information, address HarperCollins Publishers Inc., 10 East 53rd Street, New York, NY 10022.

HarperCollins books may be purchased for educational, business, or sales promotional use. For information please write: Special Markets Department, HarperCollins Publishers Inc., 10 East 53rd Street, New York, NY 10022.

FIRST EDITION

Designed by Kris Tobiassen

Illustrations by Christopher Smith

Printed on acid-free paper

Library of Congress Cataloging-in-Publication Data

Graber, Geoff, 1969–
    All in : poker night lessons for winning big at your career / Geoff Graber with Matthew Robinson.
        p. cm.
    ISBN 0-06-087348-5
    1. Success in business. 2. Executive ability. 3. Career development. 4. Poker. I. Robinson, Matthew, 1978–   II. Title.

HF5386.G6327 2005
650.1—dc22

2005051655

05 06 07 08 09 WBC/RRD 10 9 8 7 6 5 4 3 2 1

This book is dedicated to my grandfather, Papa, who taught me about poker and life.

CONTENTS

KNOW THE RULES
Dead Money

I was four years old when my grandfather taught me how to play poker. Before we sat down to play, he would take all of the low cards out of the deck, leaving only the ten through ace of each suit. Each hand my grandfather dealt me was bright and colorful, filled with pictures of fantastical kings, queens, jacks, and the very recognizable first letter of the alphabet. Each hand I was dealt was a monster hand, but my grandfather's hands were just as strong. I soon learned that two queens beat two jacks, that five cards in a row formed a straight, and that, for reasons completely unbeknownst to me, three aces were somehow better than two aces and two kings.

Although poker would eventually prove to be a complex game, demanding years of practice and dedication, my first experiences with the game were simple. More importantly, they were fun. My grandfather knew that to overwhelm me at a young age with all of the intricacies and subtleties of poker would impede any initial enjoyment I might get out of the game. You have to crawl before you can run.

Once I was comfortable playing with the high cards, he added the rest of the deck all at once. Once I understood five-card stud, we moved on to seven-card stud. In no time at all we were playing a handful of different poker games for the pennies and nickels we'd find in the couch. My grandfather understood that the key to success was to make every task simple and fun. It was the application of this very idea that has made all the difference in my life and in my career.

The process of finding the fun in everything you do is how I fell in love with cards and, later in life, how I fell in love with business. My grandfather took this big game called *poker* and simplified it so even my four-year-old mind could understand it. Getting comfortable with the basics is the first step to enjoying the game and therefore the first step to being successful at the game.

I t was only a few years ago that I was first introduced to the game of No-Limit Texas Hold 'Em. While I had been a poker player since the day my grandfather first shoved a deck of cards in front of me, I didn't become familiar with the wonderful game of No-Limit Hold 'Em until pretty late in my poker-playing life.

Once I started playing No-Limit Hold 'Em, there was no turning back. This was the poker game I had been looking for my entire life. While a lifetime of playing poker made it easy to jump in and understand No-Limit Hold 'Em, it was the complexities and the nuances of the game that kept me coming back. For the first time in my life I found myself reading poker strategy books, looking to the masters of the game to elevate my strategy and simultaneously entertain me with poker stories.

There was something about No-Limit Hold 'Em that clicked with me as no other game ever had. Something about the two cards you're dealt at the start of each hand; the community cards that all the players share to build the best hand; the strategy, both in the cards and in the players; and the unavoidable factor of luck all combined to paint a picture that just made sense to me. It all seemed so familiar. It was a game I felt naturally at ease playing, as if I had been playing it my whole life. In many ways, that feeling wasn't far off the mark.

It was within the first few months of my courtship with No-Limit Hold 'Em that I began seeing similarities between strategies I was using at the poker table and strategies I had been using at the office for years. Parallels began popping up everywhere. I realized I often "slow-played" clients in the same fashion I would slow-play pocket aces. Even the boardroom I sat in every day for meetings began to take shape in my mind as a glorified poker table, with each client and colleague having an invisible stack of chips in front of them. I noticed that some players in the boardroom had more "chips" than others, and could therefore bully the rest of the table around, while other players were running out of chips and were being forced to make careless, desperate decisions. Seeing the similarities between business and poker felt partly like a revelation, but it also felt . . . so obvious.

The more I thought about it, the more every facet of my business life began to mirror the lessons I was learning in No-Limit Hold 'Em. My career as a whole seemed to flow like a tournament lesson taken directly from T.J. Cloutier and Tom McEvoy's *Championship No-Limit & Pot-Limit Hold 'Em* (New York: Cardoza, 2004). At certain points in my career I played tightly and aggressively, waiting for the other players to knock each other out before I made any big moves. At other times in my career I have had to play some big hands and take some big risks in order to make the final table—just like a No-Limit Hold 'Em tournament.

Finding the similarities between business and poker has greatly changed my life and led to greater success in my career. Beyond that, it has taken the stressful corporate world and transformed it into an exciting and challenging poker game—a game that is built around rules and strategies; a game that can be beat. Bottom line: It has made my job *fun*. And just like my grandfather proved while teaching me thirty-odd years ago, by making something fun and simple, you make it that much easier to succeed.

Over the past few years I have taken this revelation of applying No-Limit Hold 'Em strategy to the business world, and I've expanded it into a theory that I apply daily to my career and that has improved my abilities as a player, in both business and poker, exponentially. For this book I have broken down the theory into ten simple rules that will help teach you how to make your job as fun as your weekly poker game. Beyond that, it's going to teach you how to win.

Taking a cue from my grandfather, I'm going to start off simple. We're going to start with the basics. Rule number one is *Know the Rules.*

G o to an average No-Limit Hold 'Em tournament anywhere in this country and you will invariably find a large number of amateurs playing against a small number of professional poker players. Before the tournament begins, while looking at the list of hundreds of unknowns on the tournament roster, the professionals will often comment that there is a lot of "dead money" in the tournament. What they mean by this phrase, as condescending as it may sound, is that aside from the professionals, everyone else who paid the entry fee for the tournament has simply done nothing but swell the prize purse with little or no chance of winning any of it for themselves. Before the tournament has even begun, their money is considered "dead."

While this is not always true across the board, the majority of the time it is the professional poker players who end up at the final table of any given tournament. I quote Matt Damon from the movie *Rounders* when I say, "Why do you think the same five guys make it to the final table of the World Series of Poker every year? What, are they the luckiest guys in Las Vegas?"

The difference between the pro and the dead money is that the pro has put in the appropriate amount of time honing his skills. The pro has laid the proper foundation necessary to gain a thorough understanding of poker. The pro has done what it takes to best his chances at success. Fortune favors the well-prepared poker player, and when playing cards, you always want fortune on your side. Luck has little to do with it.

The same could be said of the successful businessman. Anyone who walks in unprepared for a job interview, a deal, or a boardroom meeting is essentially dead money.

Before you learn the strategy, before you learn how to interact with the other players (in business and in poker), and before you learn the secrets that can make you a consistent winner, you have to know the rules of the game.

Before I get into how you can apply your poker skills to the business world, we need to make sure that we're all on the same page, and have a solid foundation in both. This chapter will serve as a quick lesson in No-Limit Hold 'Em as well as a crash course in poker terminology. It's important that you understand the rules of

No-Limit Hold 'Em as well as the slang of the poker table so you'll know what we're talking about in subsequent chapters when we start applying these concepts and terms to the business world.

Even if you've never played No-Limit Hold 'Em before, this chapter will set you on the path to total understanding and give you all the tools you need to have fun and to succeed. Even if you know No-Limit Hold 'Em inside and out, there's no need to skip ahead. It always helps to brush up your game, and there's a good amount of foundational strategy explained in this chapter as well.

In addition, this chapter will serve as a quick overview of what I believe to be the foundation every businessperson needs in order to survive and succeed in today's modern business world. While business as a whole doesn't have a specific, formulaic set of rules like a poker game does, there are definitely foundational concepts that are necessary for anyone looking to enter the world of business or looking to improve on a career already in progress.

That said, let's get right into it.

A SOLID FOUNDATION IN NO-LIMIT HOLD 'EM, MADE SIMPLE

No-Limit Hold 'Em, a hodgepodge of different poker games, was invented by a few of the most legendary gamblers to ever grace a card table. Men like Amarillo Slim, Johnny Moss, Titanic Thompson, and Blondie Forbes created No-Limit Hold 'Em as a poker game designed to win the largest amount of money in the least amount of time. Since the majority of these men lived in or around the Lone Star state, the game came to be commonly known as No-Limit *Texas* Hold 'Em. Yet it wasn't until Benny Binion, owner of the Binion's Horseshoe Casino in Las Vegas, began his annual World Series of Poker Championship in 1970 that the game of No-Limit Hold 'Em was introduced to the world and cemented as America's most popular form of poker.

No-Limit Hold 'Em, a game that poker legend Doyle Brunson refers to as "the Cadillac of poker," is the ultimate in high-stakes, high-swing poker. It's a game where any single hand can make or break anyone at a given table. It's a game where playing the other players at the table is as important, if not more important, than playing the cards that are in your hand. No-Limit Hold 'Em is a game where all you need is "a chip and a chair" to be a threat at any poker table. In short, it's the ultimate in strategy, concentration, and courage.

And here's how you play the damn thing.

THE TABLE

A No-Limit Hold 'Em table usually holds a maximum of ten players, but can be played with as few as two. An average game, including tournament games, will have nine players at a table. While there's no reason you couldn't have *more* than ten players at a table, most casinos have a maximum of ten per table. Playing with more than ten players can seriously slow down the flow of the game.

The Button

There are three important positions at the table. The first position is called *the button*. It is called so because at most casinos they will have a small hockey puck–shaped disk that looks like a large button in front of the player who is designated "the button" for that turn. The button signifies who the dealer is for that hand. At a casino the player with the button in front of him won't literally be the dealer—the casino will have a hired dealer who deals every hand. The button is there only to signify who the button is, the importance of which we will get to in a second. At a home game, the button is often the actual dealer because there is no permanent dealer for each hand like there is at a casino.

The Small Blind and the Big Blind

To the immediate left of the button is the *small blind* and the *big blind*. Blind just means ante (a required bet); it's an amount of money you must put up blindly, without having seen what cards you're going to get. Antes are used in No-Limit Hold 'Em to ensure that there is money in the pot at the start of each hand so that no player, aside from the big blind, can see the first three community cards without at least paying the amount of the big blind. The three positions are always immediately next to each other, three in

A poker table with the designated button (dealer), small blind, and big blind.

a row, and always in the exact same order, from right to left: the button, the small blind, and the big blind.

Of the two designated blinds, the player sitting in the big blind must pay the larger ante and the player sitting in the small blind must pay the smaller ante. The size of the blinds depends on the size of the game. Every game of No-Limit Hold 'Em has a pre-determined small and big blind amount. If you go to a casino and sit down at a $3 to $5 No-Limit Texas Hold 'Em table, that means that the small blind will be three dollars and the big blind will be five. The size of the blinds are a good indication of how much money is being played with at the table and how big each pot has the potential of becoming. A $1 to $2 No-Limit Texas Hold 'Em table will have smaller pots and less money up for grabs than a $25 to $50 No-Limit Texas Hold 'Em table, which will have big pots and players with huge chip stacks. If you've got only $100 in your pocket, you're going to want to sit at one of the smaller ante tables. Tournaments usually use an escalating blind system where the blinds double at designated periods throughout the tournament.

At the end of each hand, the button, the big blind, and the small blind positions all move one player to the left. So, if you're sitting at a table of ten players, every ten hands, the big blind followed by the small blind followed by the button will all move back around to you.

THE FLOW OF THE GAME

Each player is dealt two cards face down in front of them. These are called your *hole cards* or *pocket cards*. The player holding these cards should look at them, but they are to be kept a secret until the end of the hand. The flow of the game always follows this order: the player to the immediate left of the big blind is first to act. This player now has three options: fold, call, or raise. To *fold* your hand, often referred to as *mucking* your cards, means to toss your cards toward the middle, having decided not to play the hand. To *call* means to match the ante amount posted by the big blind. To *raise* means to raise the big blind to any amount the player so chooses. This is why the game is called No-Limit Hold 'Em: there is no limit to how much you are allowed to bet or raise. There is a minimum, though. If you stay in the hand, you must at least bet the size of the big blind for the first two betting rounds, and double the size of the big blind for the last two betting rounds.

Flow of play follows in the same fashion to the left, clockwise around the table, until it reaches the small blind. The small blind has the same options as everyone else (fold, call, raise), but since the small blind has already posted a portion of the big blind (as long as no one has chosen to raise the pot), then the small blind must pay only the remaining portion of the big blind in order to see the first three community cards.

Same goes with the big blind. If no one has yet raised the pot, the big blind can either raise the pot or say "Check," meaning the big blind doesn't want to make a raise and is ready to see the first community cards.

If anyone along the way raises the pot, all players still in the hand must call the raise in order to continue in the hand. If they think their cards aren't worth the raise, they can fold.

The Flop

With the first round of betting over, the dealer first "burns" one card, placing the card face down on the table, and then deals the first three community cards, known as *the flop*. These three cards are dealt face up in the middle of the table for all to see. The dealer always burns the top card to ensure that no player is cheating. If the top card were somehow marked or bent, a player might know what that card was in advance and change his play accordingly.

The next betting round begins, this time starting with the small blind, the player sitting directly to the left of the button. The betting round continues clockwise, each player being allowed to check (if no bet has yet been made), bet, or fold (if a bet has been made and the player chooses not to continue in the hand). If a bet has already been made, a player is allowed to raise that bet to any amount he or she deems appropriate, all the way up to going *all in* for his or her entire stack of chips.

The reason the button is considered the best position in all of Hold 'Em is that it is the last position to act in all betting rounds after the flop. Because the button is last to act, the player in that position

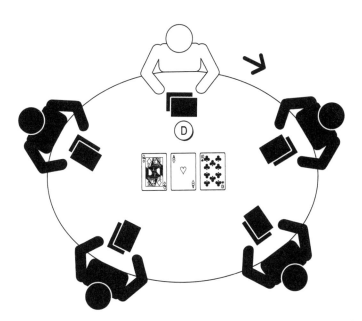

The flop. The flow of the game travels clockwise, starting with the player to the left of the button.

has the advantage of watching all the other players act before having to make a decision. The button gets the most information for free.

Fourth Street

With this round of betting over, the dealer "burns and turns" one more community card, often referred to as *fourth street* or *the turn*. With four community cards now on the table, the third betting round begins in the same fashion as the previous one, starting with the player directly to the left of the big blind and continuing clockwise around the table.

Fifth Street

Once that betting round is over, the dealer burns and turns the final community card. This card is known as *fifth street* or *the river*. A final round of betting then occurs. The players left in the hand by the end of this round have a showdown, meaning they reveal their two pocket cards and deem who has the best hand. The winner takes down the entire pot. If more than one player has the same winning hand at the showdown, then the pot is split equally among the winners.

That's how the game works. Now let's get into a bit of the strategy of the game.

PLAYING YOUR HOLE CARDS

The first stage of No-Limit Hold 'Em strategy is understanding the value of your hole cards. How to play the two cards that are dealt face down to you is the first decision you must make in each hand. There are only so many different possible combinations of hole cards you can be dealt (1,326, to be exact), and with many of the hands the values of them are obvious. The best possible hole cards

The showdown. The player in the big blind position wins the pot with an ace high straight.

are pocket aces (A-A). With A-A you have the highest possible pair going into the flop and are already a favorite to win. On the flip side, the worst possible hand is the two and the seven off-suit (2-7). Off-suit means the two cards are of different suits. The reason 2-7 is the worst hand is that you have the lowest cards possible and at the same time the cards are too far apart from each other to make a straight (five cards in a row). Also, the cards are off-suit, thus lowering your chances of a flush (five cards of the same suit).

Outside of the best and worst hands in poker you've got 1,324 other possible two-card combinations. I'm going to break them into groups to make it simple: great, good, decent, and lousy.

GREAT: A-A, K-K, Q-Q, J-J, A-Ks (the lowercase *s* stands for suited—the same suit)

GOOD: 10-10, 9-9, A-Qs, A-Js, K-Qs, A-K, J-10s, Q-Js, K-Js, A-10s, A-Q

DECENT: 8-8, 7-7, 6-6, 10-9s, K-Q, Q-10s, J-9s, A-J, K-10s, 8-7s, Q-9s, 10-8s, K-J, Q-J, J-10, 7-6s, 9-7s, A-xs (*x* means any card lower than 10), 6-5s, 5-5, 4-4, 3-3, 2-2

LOUSY: Everything else

These hole card rankings are based on statistical percentages of what hands have the highest likelihood of winning *preflop*, meaning before the first three community cards are dealt. If you were to go all in with a hand in the great category, the odds are with you that you would win more than 50 percent of the time. Of course, that means that less than 50 percent of the time you will also lose with the hands in the great category, which is why the game doesn't just stop at these two cards. If it did, every hand would be nothing but a roll of the dice with no strategy involved whatsoever.

HAND RANKINGS

It's going to take more than just your two hole cards to win a hand. You're going to have to show the best five-card hand, in any combination of your hole cards and the community cards, to win a showdown. The greater the value of your hand, the better chance you have of raking in those chips. Here's a breakdown of the hand values, which five cards beat which five cards, from weakest to strongest.

- ♣ **HIGH CARD.** Highest hole card wins. If all remaining players have hole cards *lower* than the lowest community card, they split the pot. For example, if the community cards are 10, K, J, 8, A and the two players in the hand are holding 7-5, and 4-6, respectively, then they would split the pot. Even though one of the players had a higher hole card (one player had a seven high and the other had a six high) it doesn't matter since neither of them has a card higher than any of the five community cards. Bottom line: when it comes to winning by high card, only the five highest cards in the hand count, community cards or otherwise.

♣ **ONE PAIR.** Highest pair wins, with a pair of aces as highest and a pair of twos as lowest.

♣ **TWO PAIRS.** Highest pair of the two pairs decides the winner. For example, aces and threes beat kings and queens.

♣ **THREE OF A KIND** (also known as *trips*). Three of the same card.

♣ **STRAIGHT.** Five cards all in a row, ace can be highest or lowest. For example, A, 2, 3, 4, 5 or 10, J, Q, K, A. But you can't play Q, K, A, 2, 3—ace doesn't work as a bridge.

♣ **FLUSH.** Five cards all of the same suit. Player with the highest card in their flush is the winner. For example, A, 3, 5, 9, 10 ♠ beats K, J, Q, 4, 6 ♦.

♣ **FULL HOUSE** (also known as a *boat*). Three of a kind *plus* a pair. Highest three of a kind in the full house wins. For example, A, A, A, 6, 6 beats K, K, K, Q, Q. When describing a full house you say you have "aces full of sixes" if you have three aces and two sixes.

♣ **FOUR OF A KIND.** All four of the same card.

♣ **STRAIGHT FLUSH.** Five cards all in a row, all of the same suit. Highest card in the straight decides the winner. For example, 8, 9, 10, J, Q ♦ beats A, 2, 3, 4, 5 ♦.

♣ **ROYAL FLUSH.** The *ace-high* straight flush. For example: 10, J, Q, K, A ♣. Most serious poker players will see only a few of these in their entire lives.

THE IMPORTANCE OF POSITION

What position you're sitting in at the table also plays a big role in deciding what hands you should and shouldn't play. Because the player on the button is the last to act on all rounds after the initial preflop betting round, that player has a decided advantage over everyone else at the table. As we said before, the player on the button gets to see what everyone else is going to do before he has to make any decisions of his own. Because of this, the player on the button can play a wider variety of hands than players in other positions.

Players in earlier positions to the button have to decide if they want to bet, fold, raise, or check before they've seen what the rest of the table is going to do. If a player in first position (the first player to act in the postflop betting rounds) has pocket sevens but an ace or a king comes on the flop, it would be unsafe to bet out of fear that someone with a high card has made a better pair. The player with pocket sevens might get reraised and thus have no choice but to abandon his initial raise and lose the money he has already invested. On the other hand, the player on the button with pocket sevens can easily raise the pot on the same flop if no one has yet made a bet.

The rule of position is as follows: The closer you are to the right of the button, the wider the variety of hands it is safe to play. Better position means more information, and more information means more power.

RACKING UP EXPERIENCE

Now that you have the rules and basics of No-Limit Hold 'Em down, you need to start racking up some experience. Ideally, the best way to learn is to take a pile of cash to your nearest casino and sit down and play a real, serious game with real, serious players. Since most of us can't afford to throw down real money to buffer our skills, and since I wouldn't recommend you risk your hard-earned money while learning the game, the best place to learn is online.

Most online poker sites offer play-money, full-table No-Limit Hold 'Em games with real people. This is a great way to get the mechanics of the game down while experimenting with playing styles, betting patterns, etc. Yahoo! Games—the company I work for—has a great, free No-Limit Hold 'Em site at games.yahoo.com. Not to toot my own horn, but it's a great way to learn against a pool of strong competitors. You might just find me on there as well.

Outside of online practice, I've done the majority of my learning at friendly home games. Try setting up a weekly or bimonthly poker game with a few friends. Every game have your friends bring a few people that you don't know so you can learn how to play against different people and different playing styles. Make the buy-in $20 and give everyone the same amount of chips. At the end of the night the player with the most chips takes all the cash (or you can designate the top three positions to win money). Twenty bucks a week isn't a big loss and it's a good investment in your poker education—after all, playing with real, live people in front of you is the *best* way to hone your skills.

In addition to hands-on practice, there are a slew of great poker books on the market that can quickly and vastly improve your game. In my opinion (and the opinion of most poker players), the three most important books ever written on No-Limit Hold 'Em are:

- ♣ Doyle Brunson and Allan Goldberg, *Doyle Brunson's Super System: A Course in Power Poker* (New York: Cardoza, 2002)

- ♣ T. J. Cloutier and Tom McEvoy, *Championship No-Limit & Pot Limit Hold 'Em* (New York: Cardoza, 2004)

- ♣ David Sklansky and Mason Malmuth, *Hold 'Em Poker for Advanced Players* (Henderson, NV: Two Plus Two Publishing, 1988)

While the last book on the list is more suited for Limit Hold 'Em as opposed to No-Limit Hold 'Em, I put it on the list because it's possibly the best book ever written on Hold 'Em theory, albeit a little academic for the average person's taste. Both Brunson's and Cloutier/McEvoy's books are utterly essential for any No-Limit player. If you haven't read them, pick them up immediately. If you've read them already, read them again.

You now have a basic understanding of the rules and terms of No-Limit Hold 'Em, as well as a few recommendations on how to improve your game. Now let's take a quick look at the business side of things.

A SOLID FOUNDATION IN BUSINESS, MADE SIMPLE

Regardless of where you are in your career, you can always improve on and strengthen your foundation in business. Whether you're thinking about beginning a career in business or you're fresh out of college and looking for your first job, there are certain core principles that are necessary for you to understand in order to start off your career on the right foot. It is equally important that you remind yourself of these core principles if you're looking to make the move within your company from team member to manager or if you're already a manager and looking to become the head of a division—or even a CEO.

When it comes to business, there is no perfect path. Everyone finds their own road to success, and what works for one may not work for another. Yet I believe there are three core principles a businessperson must maintain in his or her career in order to achieve success and happiness. These core principles are:

- ♣ Having passion for what you do

- ♣ Gathering experience

- ♣ Making connections with others

The best way to demonstrate the importance of these three principles is to briefly walk you through my career and show you how passion, experience, and connections have helped me to grow and to succeed.

I began my path in business in 1987 when I declared my major at UCLA in East Asian Studies with an emphasis in business— the UCLA equivalent of a business minor. As an eighteen-year-old freshman, I believed that China would eventually play a huge role in global business and I wanted to be there and be ready for it when it happened. Even though Japan was the epicenter of Asian business at the time, I believed that China had even greater potential and I liked the fact that it wasn't where everyone else was focusing their attention. In terms of global business, China was new, still relatively uncharted territory.

I started my career with passion. I learned to speak Chinese and studied Chinese culture, history, and politics. I was passionate about learning everything about China, the language and the culture. Beyond that, though, my passion was to be involved in international business. I loved traveling. I loved the idea of doing business halfway around the world. I loved the adventure of it all. I wanted to be there to bridge the gap between Chinese business and American business and to be an early player in a large market. I wanted to do something *big*. From there it was just a matter of finding a way to manifest that passion into a career. Although it wasn't the only thing I wanted to do in my career, I knew I would be able to have fun working in international business for a very long time.

This brings me to an important point: making work fun is a big part of being successful, and something that I'm going to teach you how to do in this book. Why is having fun at your job so important? Because no one can *always* win. Even the greatest players will lose big every once in a while. Therefore, if you're not having fun at work, the losses will hit harder, the successes will seem smaller, and your day-to-day life will seem like a dull, endless grind.

With this book I can teach you how to make your job fun by looking at it as a game—a game very similar to No-Limit Hold 'Em—but if you're not well suited to your line of work, then there is no chance you're ever going to have fun with it. It has to start with passion.

If you chose something you're passionate about as your career, you will have fun doing it. If you don't think you have a chance at enjoying your job, if you don't have any passion about it, it's probably time to find a different job—or even a different career. After all, if you're going to be spending ten hours a day at this thing we call *work*, then you had better be able to find enjoyment in it, or you're never going to succeed.

But passion isn't everything. You're going to need to get some experience under your belt as well. While school is a great place to learn the basics, no business textbook ever written can match the experience you'll gain from an actual job in the real world. That is why the summer following my sophomore year I began an internship at Merrill Lynch. I was working in the consumer markets division, charged with figuring out the best way to market to Chinese-American customers in the Los Angeles area. It was a great way to gather experience in business, finance, Chinese language, and Chinese culture.

Over the next few years, while still attending school full time, I had a handful of different internships and jobs in the business world, all designed to further my education and at the same time gather experience and build up my résumé. In 1990 I spent half a semester studying in Taiwan and led a project to study the Taiwan stock exchange. When I returned I began an internship at Bank of America, providing loans to Asian businesses that wanted to enter the U.S. market. This internship was particularly exciting since I was working in a brand new unit of Bank of America that was made up of only myself and one other person. It was a great opportunity to stand out and exhibit my creativity and vision.

I wrote up a marketing plan that impressed my higher-ups at Bank of America and was able to turn the internship into a part-time job working as a financial analyst. I was working twenty to thirty hours a week alongside professional businessmen and -women. At the same time I was finishing up my senior year at UCLA and attending classes in which the rest of my classmates were learning things I was actually experiencing every day. While I wasn't a full-time employee of Bank of America, I was still a full-fledged financial analyst, learning tons about finance and business and making solid connections with my coworkers and higher-ups.

At this point in my education I had one foot out the door and couldn't wait to jump into my career. I had passion for what I was doing—I was truly excited by the potential of my field of study. I was gaining experience, working in finance, and getting started in the business world. And I was making connections—getting to know the higher-ups at Bank of America, watching how my bosses operated, and learning as much as I could from them. It was be-cause of my connections in the business world that I was able to land a job at the Bank of America headquarters in San Francisco immediately following my graduation from UCLA.

Making connections is an essential part of progressing in your career. By gaining the trust and admiration of your higher-ups you stand a better chance of being promoted, and by spending time with, and learning from, the best and brightest in your field, you can grow exponentially as a businessperson. Making connections is just as much about finding mentors as it is about getting your foot in the door of as many opportunities as possible.

Fresh out of college I began working in Bank of America's high-technology lending group. Not only was this my first full-time job, but it was also my introduction to the technology field—a field that would become increasingly important throughout my career. I was immediately tasked with putting together loan pack-ages worth hundreds of millions of dollars for some of the largest technology companies in the Silicon Valley, such as Cisco Sys-tems. For the first few months it was incredibly exciting being in the technology industry, but I soon grew tired of the monotony of number crunching. I felt there were bigger and better things waiting for me elsewhere. I made sure human resources knew that they should be looking for another position for me within the company.

Luckily for me, there was a hiring freeze at Bank of America that year. In just three short months as a full-time financial analyst at Bank of America, I was able to move to the bank's venture capital group and was promoted to senior financial analyst. This was my first time working around high-tech start-ups—and I was hooked. There were only three of us running the venture capital arm of Bank of America, and together we were managing a billion-dollar portfolio. I was working with the best in my field, presenting my findings to the board, and getting the opportunity to interact with some of the most powerful men and women in finance. I felt like a kid in a candy store.

For the first few months I felt great passion for what I was doing. I was gathering some incredible experience—especially for someone of my young age—and I was making connections that would prove valuable for years to come.

Yet, even though I had an excellent job, in just a few short months my mind started to wander. I felt I was too creative for my position and it was going to take a long time for me to work my way up. Also, even though the company was strong, I did not see Bank of America as the right place for me long term. I was consumed with ideas for other projects, companies I wanted to start, and products I wanted to take to market. In short, I lost the passion for what I was doing, and I knew that without passion I would never find success or happiness. In my first "all in"–style move, I left Bank of America to chase my dreams of bigger and better things in the business world.

Over the next few years my path took a few different directions as I took on a handful of business roles, focusing on entrepreneurism, venture capital, and China. But throughout, the constant was that I was always following my passion, hungering for greater experience and searching for new connections.

I initially left Bank of America to create a start-up company around a product I called the LapSaver, a PC laptop accessory. Later, I spent some time doing start-up company consulting, which I enjoyed immensely. Then, I landed a job working for IDG (one of the world's largest publishers of tech-related magazines and books) as an associate partner in their China Venture Fund, one of the first venture capital funds in China. Because it was so early in the China market, there were very few high-tech start-ups in which to invest at the time. So, I came up with the idea of helping major U.S. companies enter China by working with them to find China-based partners, setting up local subsidiaries in the market and investing with them in the market. Luckily, I was given the opportunity to lead this new area for the fund. Among the businesses I worked with closely over the course of the first few months was Electronic Arts (EA), the world's largest video game software developer. While working with EA, helping them to see how they could be successful in the Chinese market, EA asked me to leave IDG and to come to work for them. I held out for a while, not feeling the need to leave the good thing I had going at IDG, but eventually EA's offer enticed me. In 1995 I took the job heading EA China.

EA China was my first opportunity to run a business for a larger company. It was an incredible experience in which I learned a ton and made a slew of great connections. It gave me the chance to really test myself in a new way and to also build a business from scratch in China—something I had dreamed of for many years.

In 1998 I decided to head out on my own again and work independently in the market for a few years. I once again followed my heart and partnered up with a few friends on a start-up company called Muse, a broadband Internet software company that combined rich graphics with cool multi-user web experiences. It was a great company with a lot of potential but in the end it was a technology ahead of its time, in a market that was too unstable to sustain us. After that I started working in the mobile games industry and consulted for a number of clients, including Nokia, helping them bring the N-Gage (a mobile phone for gamers) to the Chinese market.

It was in 2003 that I first began working at Yahoo!, where I was brought on to help Yahoo! expand its presence in the mobile market. While working at Yahoo! I created partnerships with many companies, including Verizon Wireless, Qualcomm, and Nokia, and grew the existing relationship with AT&T Wireless (now Cingular). These deals were great to get done and important for the company, but it was my strategy for building a mobile games business at Yahoo! that I was really passionate about. After only a short time I landed in my current position running Yahoo! Games— leveraging my passion, experience, and connections I had made in the company to win that great opportunity.

Like I said, no two paths in the business world are identical. The path you choose will look very different from mine, yet three principles have remained constant throughout my career: having passion, gathering experience, and making connections. I believe that if you maintain these three principles throughout *your* career as well, you will find your career as exciting and enjoyable as I have found mine thus far.

The more passion, experience, and connections that you have, the greater your chance of succeeding in your given field or industry. These three principles are also imperative if you want to treat your job like a game of No-Limit Hold 'Em. Without passion for what you're doing, you'll never have the same kind of fun at your job that you have at your weekly poker game. Without tons of experience in your field, you'll never have the tools needed to play with the best players and take down the biggest pots; and without making important connections in your industry, you'll never grow as a player or get invited to the big games.

With a lot of perseverance and a little luck you will be able to combine your passion, your experience, and your connections into an exciting, meaningful career that will bring you unlimited success and satisfaction. Finding that career is a lot like waiting for the right hand to play in poker: it takes a lot of patience and control. Once that perfect hand has been dealt to you, the following nine chapters are going to tell you how to play it and how to make it win big.

In this chapter we've covered the basics of what you need to know, whether it be in business or poker, before you sit down at a table with *anyone, anywhere*. Now it's time to get into the details and the strategy. Now it's time to find out how to make your job as fun and exciting as your weekly poker game. We're even going to find out how icky subjects like corporate politics can be made fun, and even better—how you can win at them.

....

THE SHOWDOWN

**Before you can make your job as fun as your
weekly poker game, you have to know the rules
and understand the foundations of both.**

....

RULE 2:

KNOW YOUR OPPONENT
Reading 'Em Blind

As a child I was far from a perfect student. The problem wasn't that I was dumb. In fact, looking back, I remember everyone around me saying what a bright kid they thought I was. The problem was that I was bored. My mind wandered in class. I couldn't find a hook to keep me interested in what was being taught. At that point in my life, all I had learned from my teachers was that I was smart enough to put in the minimal amount of effort and still skate by.

When I was six or seven years old, after bringing home a failed test, my mother sat me down and gave me one of the most important pieces of advice I was ever given.

"Just treat it as a game," she said to me. "See how well you can do and then try and do even better than that the next time."

Thinking of school as a game was just the hook I needed to make each test and homework assignment a challenging and rewarding experience.

The roots of this lay in the fact that I was part of a game-playing family. Each week my mother, father, and I would sit down and play the classic games: Clue, Risk, Scrabble, Boggle—anything we could get our hands on. We were a very competitive family and enjoyed challenging our minds and improving our strategies each and every week. More importantly, the games were a chance to learn about each other. The games themselves were incidental.

No matter what, when I sat down at that table, I was gunning for my mother and she was gunning for me (in a loving way, of course). There was nothing mean-spirited about it; we simply enjoyed playing against each other and competing each week to see who would come out on top. I would study her playing style, anticipate her next move, and adapt my playing style to disarm her—and she would do the same to me.

Aside from learning the rules of a game, I believe that the second most important rule of winning is to know your opponent. If you can quickly figure out your opponent's style of play, you can adapt accordingly and neutralize him before he (or she) has a chance to disrupt *your* style of play.

When I started my career in business I was daunted by the ruthless and intimidating nature of corporate politics. It wasn't until I realized that I could apply the same game mentality to my career as I had to my school life that I began to excel. Now I keep this ethos with me, treating each day as a series of challenges to be met and each person I encounter as a player whose style I need to quickly read and adapt to.

I n this chapter we will cover the four most common personality types you're liable to interact with in the business world and at the poker table: the Bully, Mr. Tight/Aggressive, the Wild Man, and the Chameleon.

We'll start with the play style you'll meet most frequently in the business world and at the poker table: the aggressive player, or as I like to call him:

THE BULLY

What should you do if you start a new job or sit down at a poker table to find an extremely aggressive player already there? Whether it's a colleague constantly showing you up for attention with the boss or a poker player coming over the top on every bet, there's only one surefire way to diffuse this hothead. Let's start with the poker Bully.

Poker Bully

All too often you'll sit down at a No-Limit Hold 'Em table to find one player pushing the rest of the table around, forcing the game to play at his speed and in his style. This player's aggressive betting style forces the rest of the table to play "weak/tight," meaning they play only the very best hands and fold quickly when someone bets into them, even if they had a good shot at taking down the pot.

Weak/tight is the least effective playing style possible in No-Limit Hold 'Em. A weak/tight player is one who doesn't have any confidence in his own hand, always worries that *the other guy* has the nuts (the best possible hand), and folds decent hands whenever anyone puts him to a decision for a large chunk of his chips. In other words, this is *exactly* the type of players you want with you at your table. Their chips are yours for the taking, which is *exactly* what the Bully is banking on as well.

The Bully's aggressive style of play is built on the fact that the more aggressively he plays, the faster the other players will begin playing weak/tight. How can you avoid falling into this trap? The Bully is a lot easier to contain than you think—so easy, in fact, that you'll learn to look forward to playing with the Bully.

First, you're going to adopt half of the weak/tight playing style: *the tight half*. Anytime you're in a hand with the Bully you're going to fold anything outside of great hands (big pairs, A-K; see rule 1, p. 13). This involves a lot of patience, but it doesn't mean you can't also be building your chip stack in the meantime by playing hands that *don't* involve the Bully. In fact, you can thank the Bully for giving you a table full of weak/tight players whose money is yours for the taking (as long as you don't have to go up against the Bully to get it).

Let's say you land a great hand, for example, pocket kings. The Bully bets preflop, everyone folds, and it comes around to you. What do you do? You bet big, right? Wrong. *You're not going to bet into the Bully right away.*

A big mistake a lot of players make when sitting down at a table with a Bully is to wait for the right moment to get revenge—to make the Bully feel sorry that he ever pushed anyone around. That's a big mistake. Your goal shouldn't be to anger the Bully or aggravate him further. Your goal should be to diffuse him, to get him playing defensively and *thinking* about the choices he makes against you. If you embarrass him, all you're going to do is make him bet into you even harder, making each pot you enter into with him more expensive and, thus, greatly increasing the chance of losing all your chips to him.

Instead, simply call his bet. Call it quickly and quietly. Or, if you're first to act preflop, check to the Bully, wait for him to bet, and then call the bet. If he doesn't bet, all the better for you.

No matter what happens on the flop, you're *not* going to bet. Whether you've hit a big hand or missed entirely, you're *not* going to bet. You're going to check to him. If he bets and you haven't made anything on your hand, call his bet (unless you think you're drawing completely dead, in which case you should muck it and wait for the next opportunity to try again).

By just calling or checking, you've already taken the Bully out of his playing style and gotten him thinking about what hand you have. Thoughts like "Why does this person keep calling my bets so quickly?" and "Why don't they bet back into me if they have such a great hand?" begin running through the Bully's head. Now you've got him worried.

The Bully relies on his playing style to get you playing emotionally. Whether that emotion is fear or anger, he is counting on the fact that you will either play a foolish hand in the hopes of breaking him or toss away a good hand because you're afraid of putting all your chips in jeopardy. As long as you're not playing emotionally, you've taken away the majority of the Bully's power.

Let's say the Bully didn't bet into you on the flop or the turn and you checked it through twice. The Bully only has two options now: bet into you big because he thinks you have nothing or check to you because he's afraid you're setting a trap for him. You're the one forcing him to a decision now, and all you did was check to him! If he bets into you, that's great because you played tight and probably have the better hand. Simply call his bet on fifth street and quietly take down the pot.

If fifth street hits and he *hasn't* bet into you, you may want to think about making a decent-sized bet now. As long as you think you've got the better hand and he's checked to you, betting into him is your only option. If he calls, great—you've probably got the better hand. If he folds, even better—because now he has *no idea* what type of player you are or what kind of hands you play. You'll have him worried about you, but not gunning to take you down. Rather, he'll just be hesitant to enter another pot with you.

The next time you enter a hand with the Bully he'll be less inclined to bet into you, hoping to find out what type of player you are by letting *you* make all the bets (giving you the control of the game), and when you finally *do* decide to bet into him, watch out—that bet is going to have a lot of power because of how passively you played up until that point.

A good rule to remember: Most aggressive players can't stand two checks. The Bully thrives on smelling out other players' weaknesses and will most likely make a good-sized bet after two checks *no matter what* cards they have in their hand. As long as you're playing tight, the odds are with you to win the pot. Aggression is the way of the Bully; use this to your advantage by getting him to play aggressively at the *wrong time* and with the *weaker hand*.

Once you play a few hands like this against the Bully and get him actually *thinking* about the moves he makes against you, you'll be free to loosen up your hand a bit, bet a bit more aggressively, and get back to *your* comfortable style of play.

Business Bully

When it comes to business, it's not always wrong to be the Bully. In fact, any good businessperson knows that sometimes the right move is to be extremely aggressive, even if it means coming off like a jerk.

A perfect example of a businessman who knows when and how to be the Bully is Donald Trump. Trump acts the part of the classic Bully, pushing his competitors around with his big stack of chips, jumping into markets he knows little about, like the casino market in Atlantic City, and slowly taking over the place, going up against competitors like Steve Wynn and bullying the whole town around in order to get his buildings built. Trump takes big risks, makes big bets, and likes to see how far he can push everyone who dares to play against him. Most likely, the Bully is Trump's natural playing style (a concept we'll get into more in the next chapter), but the difference between Donald Trump and your average Bully is that Trump knows when to be the Bully and when *not* to be the Bully. He uses the Bully playing style only when it best suits the situation.

The way to be the Bully and not hate yourself in the morning is to take responsibility for your actions (come to terms with the Bully within, if you will) and make peace with the fact that you're playing the role that needs to be played to get the job done. Trust me, Trump never feels bad about the fact that he has to make big bets and bully people around sometimes to get things done. It's all part of the game. That being said, here's how you handle these jerks.

Rule number one: Leave your emotions at the door. The goal of the Bully is to throw you off your game by getting your emotions involved. No one makes the right business decision when their mind is clouded by anger, jealousy, or fear. Even if the Bully doesn't realize he is playing a game (a lot of Bullies don't—it's just who they are), you must recognize the Bully for what he or she is and begin to adapt your playing style accordingly.

Just like you would at the poker table, you want to stay out of hands with the Bully as often as possible. Don't get involved with that person in deals or projects, avoid meetings with them, and generally make it your modus operandi to steer clear of them whenever possible. Whether the Bully is taking credit for work you've done or is bad-mouthing you to the boss, the only way to overcome the Bully is to isolate yourself from him or her and prove your merits on your own.

Do everything you can to let your boss give you tasks that you can do alone. Wait patiently for the opportunity to show how well you work *independently* of the Bully. Make a name for yourself by being a productive and effective member of the company, but not by self-promotion. The Bully is after attention and will consider anyone who wants to direct that attention away from him as an aggressor. The good news is that the Bully can't fault you for succeeding, so strengthen your position by building a strong foundation for yourself in the organization. Once the upper echelon says you're doing a good job, you'll have taken the wind out of the Bully's sails.

Go to your boss and say, "I think I can get these deals closed on my own. I know how busy Mr. Bully is; maybe I could help lighten his load." If your boss agrees with you, you've just taken on an independent workload that you can use to strengthen your position in the company. At the same time, you've ingratiated yourself with the Bully by offering to lighten his load.

On the other hand, if you *have* to work with the Bully, play it tightly, don't go against him or her. Remember, to act aggressively toward the Bully is to ask for aggression in return. Get by on your talents, play to your strengths, and take on only project responsibilities that you know you can nail. Or, if you have enough confidence in yourself, take a few risks in the projects you choose, but know in advance that if you fail, the first guy to point out your mistakes will be the Bully. Keep all your interactions with this person passive and you'll stay off their radar.

Most Bullies don't last very long. No one wants to deal with a Bully day in and day out. Eventually, the Bully will begin to lose accounts and word will get around about his negative attitude toward others. Sit back and be patient. If you play your cards right, you'll find yourself moving upward and onward while the Bully stays put.

Overall, use the same strategy with the business Bully that you would with the poker Bully: Patience is key; attack only when you're almost positive you have the winning hand, and keep the Bully passive whenever possible. You'll have plenty of opportunities in your career to prove your toughness; trying to prove it by going against someone who's entire game is built on toughness is the wrong move—you have to use strategy to take these players down.

This is a strategy that works well against the large number of businesspeople out there who only know how to act like the Bully. Any businessperson worth his or her salt, like any great poker player worth his or her salt, understands that you have to be able to switch up your playing style constantly if you want to be nimble enough to handle the wide variety of players you're liable to meet throughout your career. While the above strategy wouldn't work against a solid Chameleon player like Donald Trump, it would most likely force him to momentarily play in a different style and rethink his strategy against you. If possible, you always want to force an opponent off of a particular playing style by limiting that playing style's effectiveness against you.

On a side note, on the off chance that you ever end up in the nightmare situation of having a Bully for a *boss*, the best thing you can do is muck your hand and find yourself a new job. I once had a boss that constantly referred to me as "Junior" and took every opportunity possible to steal my ideas and make me look bad in the process. I made the mistake of taking the bait and yelling back at him, which only made my position with the company more volatile. The right move would have been to excuse myself from any and all one-on-one conversations with the Bully boss and to begin looking for another job. Don't let your emotions get involved, and in the meantime, begin planning your exit strategy.

MR. TIGHT/AGGRESSIVE

Whether in business or in poker, Mr. Tight/Aggressive is the style of play that I relate to the least. I'm not saying there's anything wrong with the Mr. Tight/Aggressives of the world (aside from their blatant predictability); their style of game play just isn't my cup of tea.

Mr. Tight/Aggressive takes no risks, waits patiently for only the most perfect of opportunities before acting, and is satisfied with small, unchallenged pots. These are the players who think they've found the secret to cracking the game, both in business and in poker. Put simply, they're not interested in *playing the game*. They're there to grind it out and play by the numbers. As long as they make a profit, even if it's a small one, that's enough for them.

This type of player is easily found in any company or at any casino. In fact, aside from the Bully, Mr. Tight/Aggressive is the most common player type I run into on a daily basis. While my first instinct is to advise you to find another table when you see one of these guys, often that's not an option—especially in the business world. Instead, I'm going to teach you how to tough it out, make the best of the situation, and eventually beat Mr. Tight/Aggressive.

Mr. Tight/Aggressive of the Poker Table

There's a scene in the Chris Farley and David Spade movie *Black Sheep* where Farley and Spade are playing a game of checkers together. David Spade, with a huge smile on his face, sits across from a steaming, frustrated Chris Farley.

"This is great, I never win at checkers," says Spade giddily.

Unable to take it anymore, Farley grits his teeth and blurts, "Well, it's kind of easy to win . . . WHEN YOU NEVER MOVE YOUR BACK ROW!"

That's how I feel every time I come up against Mr. Tight/Aggressive. This is the type of player who takes no risks and has no strategy (at least not a very complicated one). Mr. Tight/Aggressive plays only the best hands, bets big so everyone knows what he's got, and takes down small, insignificant pots. Rinse and repeat.

He's the type of player who makes you sit back and think, "Why are you even playing? This can't be fun for you. All you're doing is taking a seat away from someone who might actually want to *play the game*." Yet some players like playing this way. Heck, at least they're making a profit—as boring as it may be. While the tight/aggressive strategy may help you in checkers (mostly by frustrating your opponent into making mistakes), it doesn't work as effectively in No-Limit Hold 'Em, and it definitely doesn't lead to big pots and big wins.

Before we go on, let me explain what I mean by tight/aggressive play. To fold the majority of hands and wait patiently for only the great hands (A-A, K-K, Q-Q, J-J, A-Ks) is to play tightly—very tightly. To make large raises and reraises once you finally land a great hand, in order to force the other players to either fold or go all in, is to bet aggressively—very aggressively.

In a Limit Hold 'Em game the tight/aggressive play style has the potential of being very effective because Limit Hold 'Em is a much more mechanical game than No-Limit Hold 'Em. Like Blackjack, in Limit Hold 'Em if you play by the cards and the per-centages, you'll have a good chance of making some money—not a lot of money, but at least you'll have a decent shot at not *losing* all your money.

In Limit Hold 'Em you can sit back, wait for the best possible hands, hope you get some takers on your bet, and pull in a small to medium-sized pot. Grinding out the dollars is a fine way to play Blackjack and Limit Hold 'Em, but it's not how No-Limit Hold 'Em works, and it's definitely not how the business world works. In business and in poker, you're going to have to use your head a bit more and take a few risks.

So what do you do if you sit down at a No-Limit Hold 'Em table and find a tight/aggressive player playing beside you? Like I said earlier, your best bet is to find another table. If that's not an option, here's what you do.

In my opinion, having a few tight/aggressive players at your table is equivalent to playing short-handed. The only way you're going to win a pot against a tight/aggressive player is to get lucky enough to pick up a big hand at the same time he picks up a big hand and then beat him in a showdown. Even though it's a great feeling when this happens, the opportunities are few and far be-tween. Mr. Tight/Aggressive isn't going to fall for any of your tricks; he's probably not even aware that there are any tricks to fall for in the first place. He's just there to pick up a few small pots—too scared to risk any of his chips to win any real money.

The only positive thing about sitting with an extremely defen-sive player is that his blinds are as good as community property. Since Mr. Tight/Aggressive plays only monster hands, he'll most likely forfeit all of his blinds if you make any sort of preflop bet when he's on the small or big blind. While blinds won't pay the rent, I suppose it's better than nothing—although, in my opinion, it's pretty darn close to nothing. I play No-Limit Hold 'Em to win big pots, to best my opponents, to learn from my mistakes, and to have fun.

While I've said there are no real tricks you can pull against the tight/aggressive player, that isn't completely true across the board. There *is* one trick that will work against *some* tight/aggressive players. Now, don't tell anyone I told you this. Here's the big secret: *A lot of tight/aggressive players are really weak/tight players in disguise.* That's right, the more defensive a tight/aggressive player is with his chips, the more he'll be willing to muck any hand outside of the nuts, postflop.

The goal of a tight/aggressive player is to win the pot preflop by getting everyone at the table to either fold or call his great hand in the hopes that the percentages fall in his favor. He knows that any of the great hands (as long as they're not up against 50 other great hands) have better than a 50 percent chance of winning if he goes all in preflop. Just like a Blackjack player, Mr. Tight/Aggressive will double down on eleven every time and hope that the percentages work out for him. This is the right move in Blackjack. This is the *wrong* move in No-Limit Hold 'Em.

Here's the trick to playing with the weak/tight player in disguise. This takes a certain amount of gambling and a big pair of cajones, but you can call Mr. Tight/Aggressive with practically any hand and hope you get a flop that will play well against him. Ironically, in this situation you're *not* hoping your cards make a big hand on the flop, you're hoping the flop makes him think twice about the *value of his hand*. If there's a straight draw or flush draw on the table, Mr. Tight/Aggressive might become worried that his big pocket pair is no good. Most Tight/Aggressive players are so afraid of gambling and strategy that they'll muck their cards if you bet big into them after the flop, as long as the flop has the potential of making a lot of big hands. By representing that you flopped two pairs, a set (three of a kind), a straight, or a flush, you'll have a good chance of "buying" Mr. Tight/Aggressive's big preflop bet.

In my experience, this gets Mr. Tight/Aggressive very angry and causes him to storm off, miffed that his foolproof plan of winning twenty dollars per hour didn't pan out for him.

But before you try this against a tight/aggressive player you've got to make sure you've got a good read on him. Some tight/aggressive players won't let you boss them around once they've decided to enter a pot. When they play a hand, they're going to play it out and make it expensive for anyone else to play along. They do this out of fear. They want to teach the rest of the table not to get into hands with them. Why? Because they don't like taking risks. They don't like competing with other players. They don't like other people in pots with them after the flop. Before you try to make a play on the tight/aggressive player, you must make a good read on him and decide if he's the type who will play his pocket aces all the way to the river no matter what's on the board or if he's the type of player who's extremely defensive with his chips and might throw away a good hand.

Like I said, there is no trick that works against *all* tight/aggressive players, but if you can differentiate the *real* tight/aggressive players from the weak/tight players in disguise, you can pull down some big pots and get that tight/aggressive player out of his seat and away from your table. In my experience, more than half of the tight/aggressive players I've come across have actually been weak/tight players in disguise.

Mr. Tight/Aggressive of the Business World

At the poker table Mr. Tight/Aggressive isn't as much of a threat as he is an annoyance, but in the business world, a world in which you can't exactly get up and find another table to play at, the tight/aggressive player can be a real monkey wrench in your career plans.

In the business world Mr. Tight/Aggressive is the guy who is in it only for himself. The only person he cares about making a good impression on is his boss; he couldn't care less about his coworkers, the team he's on, or the company he works for. Mr. Tight/Aggressive isn't concerned with the development of his career, only his position in the company. In fact, he doesn't even care what company he works for or what industry he's in—he's happy as long as he can skate by and get that next status quo raise. In short, Mr. Tight/Aggressive of the business world never takes risks, constantly kisses up to the boss, and generally frowns upon anyone who thinks outside the box and works for the betterment of the company. I've seen these guys at almost every company I've ever worked for and they can be quite a buzz kill.

Why? Because Mr. Tight/Aggressive takes all of the excitement and energy out of almost every deal or project he becomes involved in. Mr. Tight/Aggressive is so concerned with the risks involved in each business scenario that he loses focus and becomes obsessed with how a particular deal or project might potentially effect him negatively. Basically, they take the wind out of everyone's sails and have the potential to seriously stifle a group or company's creativity.

In the short term, Mr. Tight/Aggressive might be able to make a good impression, but it's only because he's an expert at telling the boss exactly what he or she wants to hear. In the long term, Mr. Tight/Aggressive doesn't last. He's not a tournament player—

mainly because he's not playing the game at all. Any good manager should be able to see through this guy pretty quickly and send him packing.

Mr. Tight/Aggressive will never come up with the creative ideas, he's never going to take the big risks, and he's definitely never going to be the guy leading your organization in the future. This is a good thing because he's taken himself out of the competition, but the downside is that he's not a team player. Just like at the poker table, Mr. Tight/Aggressive of the business world is simply taking a seat from another player who could actually be *playing the game.*

Having Mr. Tight/Aggressive as a colleague can be a real pain in the ass. There's nothing worse than a player who always avoids conflict with you while constantly kissing up to the boss. If both of you have a shared project to work on, the only thing Mr. Tight/Aggressive is going to be concerned with is appeasing the boss. He'll say to hell with the project and to hell with getting it done as a team. If he can slip out of the work and appease the boss, then he'll feel he's done the right thing. If he can make you look bad in the process, thereby making himself look better in the eyes of the boss, all the better for him. Mr. Tight/Aggressive never gets the work done, and yet the boss always thinks he's doing a great job because he "manages up" constantly. This type of player has all the excuses in the book and isn't a team player at all.

I once was sent on a business trip with a tight/aggressive colleague, and during that trip I learned a lot about what it is that makes Mr. Tight/Aggressive play the way he plays. In short, Mr. Tight/Aggressive is scared. These types of players don't like confrontation and they're scared of taking risks. I found that by engaging Mr. Tight/Aggressive, getting him involved in as many aspects of your project or business plan as possible, you can sometimes bring Mr. Tight/Aggressive out of his shell a bit. While this doesn't work for all tight/aggressive players—some of them have such giant walls built up around them that you'll never be able to draw them into the game—it's always worth a try to attempt to draw this player out and get him playing the game.

Mr. Tight/Aggressive is simply nervous or fearful about his future. If given a bit more responsibility or a greater leadership role, this player might feel more in control of his destiny and could possibly be willing to take a few more risks. Making Mr. Tight/Aggressive feel trusted as a colleague might cause him to be less paranoid about working as a team player. Just like at the poker table, do whatever you can to draw (bait) this player type into playing the game. Make him feel like a better player, make it easier for him to enter hands, and you might just find that Mr. Tight/Aggressive will begin to play a bit looser, thus increasing your opportunity to win large pots.

Never dismiss the tight/aggressive player right off the bat. Give him or her a shot. If this player is not on your team, think about adding him or her to your team. There can be some advantages to having a tight/aggressive player on your team, as long as you are able to draw him or her into the game a bit. First off, Mr. Tight/Aggressive is a very loyal player. He doesn't like to move around too much in his company; he wants stability at all times. If he's working for you or with you, chances are he wants to keep it that way and will be loyal to you because of that. Mr. Tight/Aggressive is the guy who never leaves. You'll often hear people in the hallway commenting on how they can't believe "that guy is still here." Mr. Tight/Aggressive can often outlast everyone—not because of his skill, but because of his ability to manage up and always make himself look good to the higher-ups, and at the same time stay under the radar. Mr. Tight/Aggressive just kind of floats by.

One good reason to try and draw Mr. Tight/Aggressive into the game a bit, or at least get him on your side, is that because of his loyalty, Mr. Tight/Aggressive can be a very strong ally. Whether you like the guy or not, it's always beneficial to have an ally. Whether that ally is a client, works within your own company, or works for someone else, you never know when a friendly connection might come in handy. Most people simply dismiss the tight/aggressive player, considering him a brown-noser and a nuisance. This only pushes the tight/aggressive player deeper into his paranoid state. As simple as it sounds, try and befriend the tight/aggressive player—you might end up with a great soldier in the trenches.

If none of your attempts to draw Mr. Tight/Aggressive into the game work, and you find yourself unable to befriend him, your best move is to get involved with him as rarely as possible. Because of his tendency to make you look bad in front of the higher-ups he can be a real danger to your career. If you have to work with him on either a project or a deal, make sure you only bring your A-game. Just like playing the Bully, you want to only play your best hands against Mr. Tight/Aggressive. The only way to show up Mr. Tight/Aggressive is to make it obvious to the higher-ups that you were the one who landed the client or closed the deal. Anytime you work closely with a tight/aggressive player you have to make it obvious that all of the successes came directly from you. Just like at the poker table, if you can't bait Mr. Tight/Aggressive into loosening up his game, you're going to have to beat him with a very strong hand.

THE WILD MAN

The next most commonly found player type embodies the worst aspects of the Bully and Mr. Tight/Aggressive combined into one person. He is wildly aggressive *and* has no interest in strategy. I call him the Wild Man—the player who has absolutely no idea what he's doing and doesn't even care to learn.

The Wild Man is the player who shows up in the boardroom or at the poker table and acts without cause or reason. Whether he's emulating a play style he saw on television or he's just going on pure gut instinct, the Wild Man is nearly impossible to get a good read on. After all, how can you anticipate the next move of an opponent who barely knows what he's doing himself?

While most players will tell you that your best move is to get out of the Wild Man's way and let him self-destruct, don't run so fast—there may be a method to his madness. Whether in business or in poker, the following section will give you some tried-and-true tactics to counteract this wildly erratic, seemingly chaotic playing style.

The Poker Wild Man

The Wild Man is the guy at the poker table tossing in chips with both hands, trash talking nonstop, and pulling out miracle wins on the river. He's the player who goes all in on pocket aces *and* J-4 off-suit. No matter who plays against him, he seems to constantly pull out huge wins.

You've been watching him for a few hands. You know he has no idea what he's doing. You know he's a horrible player. You know he's just getting lucky. He just won a pot with a Q-3 off-suit by catching a queen on the river, for crying out loud! It's infuriating. You want to take him out. You want to see him walk out of the room with his head hanging low. But then you remember you're a *real* card player. You don't let your emotions get the best of you.

While the Wild Man may win a few big pots here and there, in the long run he'll lose just as many. Yet these are the types who always seem to have a big stack of chips piled in front of them, their faces all aglow in confidence. Why? Because the Wild Man doesn't stick around at the table after he's taken a big loss. The Wild Man plays purely on adrenaline and emotion. If you find this type at your table, most likely he's on a rush or lucky streak that won't lost long. Once his rush is over, his confidence is blown and his chips are gone . . . and so is he.

The Wild Man plays to teach the world that nobody pushes him around! He's got the world's biggest chip on his shoulder, and when he gets embarrassed and loses his whole stack he goes storming out of the room, dragging that big chip behind him. Good riddance. Your goal is to facilitate this inevitable ending as quickly as possible by getting him up and away from your table, and hopefully by being the one to relieve him of his chip stack in the process.

For the most part you'll find the Wild Man playing at the lower-ante No-Limit Hold 'Em games. Aside from having fewer pros and experienced players at the lower-ante tables, a lot of tight/aggressive players play these lower-ante tables as well. The Wild Man does very well against a table full of tight/aggressive players. He's able to steal their blinds, bluff like crazy, and take a lot of pots—a lot of *small* pots, that is. After all, Mr. Tight/Aggressive bets only when he's got a big hand, which usually baits the Wild Man into calling, losing his whole stack, and storming out of the room. They're a match made in heaven.

A lot of the Wild Man's effectiveness lies in his table presence. Having a decent-sized stack in front of him and taking down a high number of pots, albeit small ones, can give some people the impression that he is a winner, that he might even be a formidable opponent. This image can cause some players to fold hands they wouldn't normally fold. It can also cause some players to let their emotions get the best of them and to play hands they wouldn't normally play. Rule number one when dealing with the Wild Man is to check your emotions at the door. While this should *always* be your rule regardless of whom you're playing against, some people need an extra reminder when it comes to the Wild Man. After all, it's not easy to watch a bad player take down pots on the river with hands he should never have been playing in the first place. And then to have to listen to him gloat about it! It's almost too much. Just tune it out and stick to the plan.

The plan goes as follows:

Your first step is to tighten up by playing only strong hands. While you don't have to tighten up your play quite as much as you would against Mr. Tight/Aggressive, you're going to want to limit your play to hole cards in the great and good groups only (see p. 13, for group listings).

While the Wild Man usually plays substandard hands, you still don't want to get into a "coin toss" situation with him. You want to go in with hands that are most likely a big favorite against the types of hands he usually plays. Since you know he's the type to play pretty much any face card no matter what the kicker is (the kicker being the lower card of your two hole cards, or the card in your hand that hasn't made a pair on the board), you want to make sure you always have at least a pocket pair or a face card with a *high* kicker—a ten or higher. Your goal isn't to gamble *with* him; your goal should be either to make him gamble a bit *less* when you're in the pot, or, if he can't learn that lesson, to lose all his chips to you and to leave.

Once again, don't give in to the temptation to play cards such as pocket sevens against him. You'll probably say to yourself, "Man, he plays with garbage and puts so much money in the pot. I know I can take him with these pocket sevens." And maybe you can, but it's going to cost you a lot of chips to find out and you never know what crazy cards the Wild Man might be playing with. You want to make sure that if he's going to beat you, he better have a great hand or a lot of luck. Either way, the odds are with you in both cases, and that's the best you can ask for.

It's ironic but you almost have to become Mr. Tight/Aggressive to put the Wild Man in his place. This can lead to some boring, patience-testing poker, but luckily for you, he's not the only player at the table (hopefully). There are still plenty of other players you can unleash your true game on, but against the Wild Man you need to keep it tight/aggressive.

Also, if possible, do what you can to ensure heads-up play against the Wild Man. Isolate him from the other players. You don't want anyone else coming into the hand when you're playing against the Wild Man. Your goal is to have better cards than he has and to call or check-raise him the whole way through. This style of play doesn't work as well in a multiway pot, so make sure you bet or raise enough before the flop to scare the rest of the table away. As long as you've got a hand in the first two groups ("great" and "good" groups), you've most likely got a better hand than the Wild Man and will be in a great position to win the pot.

Another trick that works well against the Wild Man is to use his fragile emotional state to your advantage. Since you know he is the type of player who responds emotionally to a direct challenge, try check-raising him with your great or good group hands. If you have the opportunity to check to him, wait for him to raise, then come over the top with a huge raise, maybe even give him your best "bring it on" face while you do it, and he'll most likely play more stupidly than he usually does. You might even get him to stay in a hand when he's drawing dead, meaning there's no card in the deck that could possibly improve his hand beyond the strength of yours. Check-raising and winning a huge pot from the Wild Man usually sends him running for the door in frustration or puts him fully on tilt.

This brings me to an important point: The Wild Man is basically a guy just about to go on tilt. A phrase borrowed from the pinball world, *tilt* means to self-destruct by playing 100 percent with one's emotions. When a player loses a big hand and then immediately plays the next hand (or hands) with reckless abandon in the hopes of quickly winning that money back, then that player has gone on tilt.

Because the Wild Man's style of play is an emotional one to begin with, he's never far from going on tilt. While check-raising a good player can make him player *better* poker against you, it has the opposite effect on the Wild Man. Check-raising the Wild Man puts him on tilt and causes him to play his worst poker against you. Once you've check-raised him to a big loss and put him on tilt, you can loosen up your hand selection to include the decent group of hands. Now go in for the kill. If he's on tilt, the odds are with you that he's playing with trash hands. That doesn't mean that *you* should play stupidly by playing the kind of hands he would play, but you can feel free to loosen up your hand selection a bit. See you later, Wild Man.

The Business Wild Man

Let me cut right to the chase: the Wild Man can be a total disaster in the workplace. He is a player who acts out frequently. In meetings he has a tendency to speak out of turn, to waste time on topics that relate only to him, or to blow his top, seemingly for no reason whatsoever. This is the kind of guy who causes his boss to turn to someone on his team halfway through a meeting and whisper, "Who the hell is this guy?"

The Wild Man does what he wants and thinks the rules are meant to be broken. He's the type of player who, if a rule or project or idea doesn't make sense to him right away, decides that the rule or project or idea is just plain stupid—and makes sure everyone around him knows how he feels. The Wild Man makes decisions without caring about the consequences. He'll throw away decades of company protocol without stopping to consider if he's possibly throwing the baby out with the bathwater. He's often reckless for the sake of being reckless, obnoxious for the sake of being obnoxious, and aggressive for the sake of being aggressive.

While at first the Wild Man may come off like the one guy at the company who is going to stir everything up, possibly get the company moving in a whole new direction, often the Wild Man has no idea what he's doing and is flying purely on autopilot. He makes his decisions with his emotions and has a tendency to try and destroy anyone who encroaches on his territory. He's got a huge ego and he's ready to fight to the last man any chance he gets to protect it.

I know what you're thinking: the Wild Man sounds like my boss. Well, you're not far off. A lot of CEOs are Wild Men. A lot of VPs are Wild Men. A lot of managers are Wild Men. Guys who play big, swing for the fences, and make a big noise are often the ones who get promoted very quickly. Just as in poker, you'll either find the Wild Man sitting with a big stack in front of him or you won't find him at all. The Wild Man has a tendency to impress the top brass very quickly, often in just one or two meetings. He gets them thinking thoughts like "This guy is no nonsense," "This guy's got passion," "This is the type of guy I want fighting for me out there every day!"

But does the Wild Man have what it takes to back up these expectations? Or is he nothing but hot air? There's no definitive answer to that question, but I'd say that the majority of Wild Men I've come across have a hard time harnessing their own passion and energy into a consistent and positive work flow. They may have a few good years, but sooner or later they won't come through and that's the end of the road for that Wild Man. That is, until he resurfaces at yet another company and starts the whole process over again.

You'll find a lot of Wild Men helming start-up companies. These guys are great at getting investors excited about their products. They're great at putting together a big chunk of investment very quickly. They're great showmen and top-notch sellers, but many times their start-ups fall apart because of nearsightedness or their lack of attention to detail. After all, a company can't survive on passion alone. It needs hard work, know-how, and patience—three skills the Wild Man usually lacks.

But like I said, these guys can often make their way to the top very quickly, based solely on their charisma and their passion. The Wild Men who are able to mellow out a bit once they achieve that high position are the ones that go on to become great businessmen and top-notch CEOs. After all, passion is extremely important in business. It's something you simply can't fake. You've either got it or you don't—and the Wild Man has it in spades. If I were going to start with only one trait as a businessman and have to learn all the others from scratch, I would want to start off with passion.

I relate heavily to the Wild Man. At my core, I have a lot of the Wild Man's tendencies (which we'll get into more in the next chapter). I've been known to throw away the rule book if it doesn't seem to work for me. My management style is to pitch things at the wall and see what sticks. If an idea doesn't seem to benefit my team or my company, I toss it without thinking twice. Now, at this point in my career I've learned to harness the Wild Man within me to the point where it doesn't get me into trouble anymore (for the most part), but I'm constantly finding new ways in which the Wild Man emerges from within and causes me to act rashly. I've learned to deal with the Wild Man within by always "soundboarding" my ideas before I act on them. I always bounce my ideas off at least one person before making a big decision just to make sure I'm not doing something completely reckless or off the wall. I know I have a tendency to act quickly, passionately, and emotionally; I'm aware of my ability to act impulsively, without thinking about the consequences; and therefore I make sure I check myself before every decision I make.

This is pretty much how you have to deal with the Wild Man in your office as well. It's all about harnessing the strengths of the Wild Man while helping him to control his weaknesses. If you're a team leader and find a Wild Man on your team, the best way to control him is to make sure he always runs every idea by you. It's best not to completely shut down any idea he has, as the Wild Man has a tendency to act out when he feels his talents are being limited by the higher-ups. If you like his idea, greet it with great praise. If you don't like his idea, find a way to incorporate his skills in another project, or find a way to turn the idea you didn't like into an idea you do like. Remember, the Wild Man runs on passion, if you keep him feeling passionate and give him ways in which to express his ideas, you'll have a strong, creative, and often visionary addition to your team.

If you have to work with the Wild Man as a colleague on a project or a deal, your best chance at turning him into a beneficial partner is to be honest and open with what you believe to be his weaknesses and his strengths. If you're going into a meeting with him, let him know that he's best at showing the "vision" of the product or deal you're pitching. When it comes to making the client feel confident and secure in taking on your business and all the details that come with it, make sure the Wild Man knows that you believe this isn't his strong suit. If you're met with confrontation when you try to reason with the Wild Man, as you often will, it's best to simply get out of his way and let him fall on his ass. There's not much you can do, and it's the best way for the Wild Man to learn. Similarly, at the poker table, if I can't get the Wild Man to play a little bit tighter, I'll work to feed him a big loss and hope that teaches him to reign in his careless play style.

If you've got a Wild Man for a boss or CEO, you're in for a wild ride. You're either with a team or company that is truly going to make some waves in your industry or within your company, or you're with a team or company that's going to have a new boss or CEO very soon. The Wild Man is either a big success or a big failure — he rarely walks the line of mediocrity or moderation.

THE CHAMELEON

Taken individually, the three playing styles we've covered in this chapter are good examples of who *not* to be at the poker table or in the business world. But does that mean you should *never* play aggressively and loosely like the Bully? Does that mean you should never sit patiently and guard your chips defensively like Mr. Tight/Aggressive? Does that mean the Wild Man is always inappropriate at every poker game or in every business situation? Not at all.

Most players, in business and in poker, make the mistake of honing only *one* specific style of play. They pick a style they feel comfortable playing with at an early stage in their career and try to subtly improve on it throughout their lives. They never realize that each play style becomes advantageous only when applied against the right players and at the right time in the game.

The reason I'm able to give you tips on how to neutralize the Bully, Mr. Tight/Aggressive, and the Wild Man is that at their essence, they're extremely predictable. It's amazing how often I still find these types of players both at the poker table and in the world of business. Not a day goes by that I don't come across at least one of these three types of players. You'd think they would have figured out how predictable they are by now! Oh well, all the better for you. If only these players knew how much more effective they would be if they switched up their game play a bit throughout the course of game.

Aside from teaching you how to handle certain player types and to neutralize them, this chapter also serves as a guide to *understanding* how these player types function and to what capacity, and in what situations, they are effective. Anyone who plays *exclusively* with these styles is an easy target and a guaranteed loser in the long run. The player who understands these playing styles and knows how and when to use them can, and will, play with the best of them. I call this player the Chameleon.

The Chameleon has no set style of play. He understands the importance of never becoming predictable and always keeping one's opponents guessing. The minute the Chameleon feels someone has picked up on the style in which he's playing, he switches it on them. The Chameleon is always one step ahead of the game. He is able to adapt to any situation and has an instinctive feel for the flow of game play. Chameleons become killer poker players. Chameleons become great CEOs.

Bill Gates is an excellent example of the pure Chameleon. When the moment is right to play the Bully, such as when the justice department was coming down on him, he plays the Bully. When the moment is right to be Mr. Tight/Aggressive, to wait out untested tech trends and simply stick to what Microsoft knows best—operating systems—and let other businesses self-destruct on their own, then he becomes Mr. Tight/Aggressive. Or even when it's time to take a big leap and a huge risk by entering the video game market with the Xbox—a market that was practically owned by Sony and Nintendo—and to not only hold his own but become an innovator and a trendsetter within that market, then he becomes the Wild Man. That's what it takes to be a Chameleon.

Virtually every successful, well-known CEO working today is a full-fledged Chameleon. If you've heard of them, if they've achieved great success, it is because they're Chameleons. Players who cultivate only one single style of play never make it to the top of the pile; instead, they get weeded out slowly or rise only as high as their potential allows.

Chameleons know no boundaries and therefore break new ground within their particular field and industry constantly. Chameleons are players like Yahoo!'s Terry Semel, GE's Jack Welch, Microsoft's Bill Gates, Apple and Pixar's Steve Jobs, Donald Trump, Dell Computers' Michael Dell, Virgin's Richard Branson, and Ebay's Meg Whitman, just to name a few. But outside of the truly famous businessmen and businesswomen of today, there are Chameleons in almost every company. Any player who knows how to adapt to any situation or player, who understands the importance of having a wide array of playing styles in his or her arsenal, and is able to innovate and stretch within the field or industry in which he or she works is a true Chameleon.

Aside from teaching you how to make your job as fun as your weekly poker game, one of my goals in this book is to give you all the tools you need to become the Chameleon. Yet there are no easy paths to becoming the Chameleon—it takes dedication, patience, and experience. The ten rules in this book will lay the groundwork for becoming a great player in business and poker, but only dedication and years of hard work will turn you into a perfectly adaptable player with a finely tuned instinct for the flow of the game.

Therefore, my advice for handling the Chameleon is as follows: *watch and learn.* Unless you are as experienced or as instinctive a player as the Chameleon, you are simply outmatched. My best advice is to sit back and watch him play. Notice how he reacts to different players and different play styles. Study the way in which he takes control of the game at certain times and at other times takes a backseat and lets the other players take control. While you may win a few pots against the Chameleon, in the long run (or in a tournament) the Chameleon will usually prevail. At least, the Vegas odds are always with him.

So what happens when two or more Chameleons come face to face at the poker table or in the business world? Well, you're in for quite a show. The final table of the World Series of Poker is usually a good example of this. Or take a look at the battle between Steve Jobs and Bill Gates that has been going on for a few decades and will probably go on for years to come. You can learn a lot just watching two Chameleons face off against each other, either in business or in poker. While Chameleons enjoy the challenge of facing off against each other, the majority of them are glad they don't have to do it too often. A world full of Chameleons would be a pretty tough place to make a living.

There are no real strategies one could implement against a Chameleon, since in many ways he is as perfect a player as possible. Following is a list of traits that define a Chameleon so you can at least better prepare yourself for spotting one in a crowd.

TRAITS OF THE CHAMELEON

- ♣ Constantly adapting to new challenges

- ♣ Always watching and reading opponents

- ♣ Great personal control

- ♣ Enthusiastic competitor

- ♣ Focused and patient

- ♣ Great interpersonal skills

- ♣ Intense thirst for knowledge

- ♣ Calm, cool, and collected

- ♣ Love for the game

While becoming the Chameleon should be a major career goal, everyone has to start somewhere. The next chapter will help you figure out what playing styles are most comfortable for you, how and when to switch up your playing styles on the competition, and how all of this will eventually add up to making you a very agile and adaptable opponent, just like the Chameleon.

....

THE SHOWDOWN

By studying the three main types of opponents you're liable to meet in both business and poker— the Bully, Mr. Tight/Aggressive, and the Wild Man—you'll be well on your way to becoming the Chameleon—the perfect player.

....

RULE 3:

DEFINE YOUR PLAYING STYLE
The Stranger

A friend of mine recently returned from a local poker tournament in the San Francisco area and regaled me with this tale of poker woe. He and I are similar poker players, evenly matched in skill and experience, and we play with each other often. While I'm not a big tournament player, mostly because I'm too busy to take a whole day off to play cards at a casino, I related to his story so intensely that I felt it served as a perfect example of the importance of understanding one's playing style. I won't use his real name, since an embarrassing tournament loss isn't something most people like to have put down in writing for all eternity. I'll call him Jim.

This was Jim's very first No-Limit Hold 'Em tournament. It

was a small, $50 buy-in tournament with fewer than 500 players registered. During the first hour of the tournament, players who lost all of their chips were allowed to rebuy as many times as they wanted for another fifty bucks. A rebuy allows you to enter back into the tournament with the same amount of chips you started with. It's like putting another quarter into an arcade machine and giving it another go. Lots of tournaments use the rebuy system because it swells up the prize money while making the first hour of game play a bit more exciting.

The only penalty for losing all of your chips in the first hour of the tournament is that you have to pay another fifty bucks to try again—a pittance compared to the thousands of dollars up for grabs to the players who make it to the final table. Because of this, most players play recklessly during the first hour, taking big stabs at pots they'd never usually chase in the hopes of doubling up their chip stack and getting in good position for the *real* part of the tournament: everything *after* the first hour.

When it came to tournament experience, Jim had none, yet he felt completely comfortable at his first table that day. Because of the rebuy system, everyone was playing wildly and aggressively, attempting to double up their chip stacks, unafraid of losing it all since the worst case scenario was that they'd spend another fifty bucks to try again. Luckily for Jim, wild and aggressive is his natural play style. It's his comfort zone. He can toss chips on the felt with the best of them. The minute Jim sat down he started doing what he always does when he sits down at a poker table: he bullied the table around, played extremely loosely, and went with his gut on almost every decision. On that particular day, luck was on Jim's side and he was able to double up, not once, but *four times* before the first hour was up. By the time he was shifted to another table he had one of the biggest stacks in the tourney.

Unfortunately, that would be the high point of the day for Jim. Up until that point, his wild/aggressive play style had put him at the top of the pack. Everyone else at his table was playing pretty tightly, well aware that he was going to put them to a big decision for all of their chips every time they entered a pot with him. Jim was on a winning streak, "rushing" as they call it, and he completely lost sight of the big picture: *winning the tournament.* It never occurred to him that he ought to slow down, tighten up his hands, and wait for the small stacks to knock each other out. Jim had the typical "if it ain't broke, don't fix it" mentality. While this mentality may work well for toasters, it doesn't apply to much else in life.

The rest of the table quickly adapted to his Wild Man playing style and used it to their advantage to trap him into playing bad hands. Before Jim knew it, he had one of the smallest stacks at the table and was easy prey for better opponents who could take stabs at his stack whenever they wanted to. Jim lasted for only another hour and a half, finishing well outside of the money.

When he walked away from that tournament, his mind was flooded with "*if only*" thoughts: *If only* he had taken a moment to stop and think about how he was playing in relation to the rest of the tournament. *If only* he had relaxed for a moment and taken stock of his opponents. *If only* he had taken a reality check.

Several times in my business career I've reached my limitations—at least what I believed my limitations to be at the time. Several times in my career I've felt as though my personality and my experiences were limiting my growth. I hoped that somewhere, deep inside, the potential for further growth existed, but I knew that in order to find that out I would have to change considerably. I knew that I would have to rethink this whole concept of who I was. Whether it was because of certain personality traits, issues of control, or just plain old fear, somehow I was holding myself back.

Everyone hits this point sometime in their career. It's inevitable. You will hit a wall. At some point, everyone will reach their perceived personal limitations and have to decide whether they want to make a big change in order to move on to that next level or stay where they are. I've hit this point several times in my career, and each time I've decided it was important for me to do whatever it took to make that next step. Each time I've hit that wall I've chosen to challenge myself to go beyond my comfort zone and to play outside of my natural playing style.

This brings me to an important point: Everyone has a natural style. Whether you're aware of it or not, *you've* got a natural style. Whether it's your first time at a poker table or your first time at a job interview, everyone has a style that they feel more comfortable with than any other style. For some, their natural style is what they call home, relying on it day after day, for every decision they make. For others, their natural style comes out only in times of stress, a crutch on which they fall back in moments of great pressure. Then there are those people who understand their natural style and use it only when the timing is right, relying instead on a whole spectrum of other playing styles to help guide them through life's obstacles. I call these people the Chameleons. Everyone has a natural style; it's not a bad thing—it's what you're comfortable with. But if you stick to just one style your entire career, you'll end up just like Jim did in his first tournament: walking away with a head full of *if only* thoughts.

In the last chapter we covered four of the most commonly found styles in business and poker, and we covered the most effective strategies for neutralizing each one of them. I focused mainly on the negative aspects of the Bully, Mr. Tight/Aggressive, and the Wild Man, accentuating their weakness and exposing their vulnerabilities. Yet, making use of one of these three playing styles isn't *always* the wrong move. The problem comes from using *only* one of these three playing styles.

In fact, I believe everyone can trace their natural playing style back to one of these three character types. While some players may not be quite as defensive as Mr. Tight/Aggressive or as aggressive and unpredictable as the Wild Man, I believe that each and every player, in both business and poker, can find the roots of their natural playing style in one of these three character types. It's the players who learn to use *all three* of these playing styles, in all of their varying shades and subtleties, who become agile, competitive players. These are the players who become Chameleons.

As I've said before, the great players of the world are

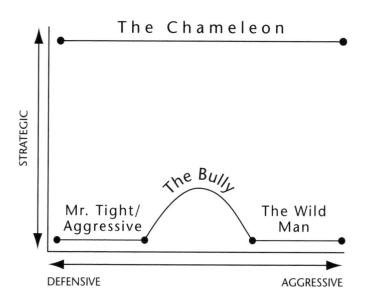

Chameleons. They have a cool confidence about them because they've been through it all. There's no cockiness to them, they're just relaxed. You find this in the great CEOs and poker professionals of the world. Doyle Brunson has such confidence in himself that he was able to put out a book revealing all of his poker strategies to the world and yet still continues to win big games to this day. The Chameleons of the world don't have a natural playing style anymore; they're comfortable playing in all situations—but they had to start somewhere.

How do the Chameleons of the world adapt so easily to each situation? What goes on in their heads when they make a decision? What may look like pure gut instinct to the outsider is actually a complex combination of situational analysis and vast experience. While not everyone can play as perfectly as the Chameleon, we can all learn a lot from the Chameleon's thought process and, by doing so, improve our own game play vastly.

In this chapter we will break down the Chameleon's thought process. We'll slow it down so we can see how the gears turn and how the decisions are made. By doing this we will gain a better understanding of who we are, why we make the decisions we make, and how we can improve ourselves as players. Understanding your own playing style is the first step to moving beyond your natural abilities and unleashing your true potential. We'll end this chapter by showing, step by step, how a reality check would have helped Jim and possibly spared him the embarrassment of an early tournament loss, and how reality checks can help you move up in the business world.

I n poker, the Stranger is a player who shows up at a poker table a complete mystery to everyone—a total unknown. The Stranger is the player you have to watch for a few hands before you know how to play against him.

For the moment, I want you to pretend that *you* are that Stranger. You've never seen this person before, you have no idea how he or she plays. It's time to sit back and take a good, long look at who exactly this Stranger is.

THE REALITY CHECK

Every hour of every working day a little alarm goes off on my PDA (personal digital assistant). No, it's not a reminder to pick up my dry-cleaning on the way home; it's a reminder to take a reality check. Five days a week, every hour on the hour, I ask myself the following five questions, couched in poker terminology:

1. What is your natural style of play?

2. How big is your chip stack?

3. What are your strengths and weaknesses?

4. What's your table image?

5. What's it going to take to leave feeling like a winner?

By asking myself these five questions, every hour of every working day, I make sure that I always have my wits about me, that I stay on course, and that I'm consistently playing the best I can play.

You see, I'm not very self-reflective by nature. Meditating on life and thinking about *why* I do *what* I do was never something that came easily to me. In fact, I fought the idea of taking a daily reality check almost every step of the way in my life. It's just not something most people like to do, and I'm no exception. But I reached a point in my career where, in order to take that next step, it was something I *had* to do. I felt that I had no choice but to take a good, long look at *who I was* in order to become *who I wanted to be.*

It helped me to put it all into poker terminology. The reality check is something that I've learned to do from applying poker strategy to my business life. In order to stay sharp, agile, and in a good position to win, I had to remind myself to take one moment each hour to think about how I was playing, how my opponents were playing, and what changes I needed to implement in order to stay strong in the competition. From there it was a natural progression to begin applying the same reality check to my career. The results were phenomenal.

Today, I view the reality check as a game strategy that is necessary in order to play in the big leagues. Let me take you through the process.

Question 1: What Is Your Natural Style of Play?

When I was a kid, breaking the piñata was a very popular birthday party pastime. At every birthday party one could gleefully anticipate the moment when a parent would come walking out with a candy-filled papier-mâché monster dangling from their hands. That parent would then tie the monstrosity to a tree branch, blindfold the first hyperactive child in line, and apprehensively hand over a plastic baseball bat to this now *blind and weapon-wielding third grader.* Whoever thought up this game was insane.

I learned at an early age that the kid who actually broke the piñata, sending the candy spilling all over the ground, was also the last kid to start picking up the candy and, therefore, at the end of the spectacle, the kid with the least amount of candy. The time it took to remove one's blindfold and toss one's plastic bat to the ground was, coincidentally, exactly the amount of time it took for the other candy-starved children to snatch up the best candy, leaving you with only Smarties and Tootsie Rolls to gnaw on. Noticing this, I formulated a strategy.

When it was piñata time, I would place myself in the first third of the line, giving plenty of time for the piñata to get nice and loosened up by the first few bat-wielding children. When it was my turn at bat I would swing just hard enough *not* to break the piñata but to make sure that the next kid in line would *definitely* break it. After my perfectly weighted swing pushed the piñata to the edge of bursting, I would secretly and quietly wait in pre-pounce position for the candy to come pouring out when the next kid struck the piñata. I was the only one who knew when the candy was coming and therefore was always in the best position to get the best candy. And I *always* got the best candy. Always.

Now, don't get me wrong. I wasn't an evil, calculating child. I didn't care about the candy very much at all. In fact, I always passed the majority of my candy out to the other kids just to show them I was a good sport. What I cared about was winning. Winning for the sake of winning.

I was a very competitive child. But I was also a risk taker. I knew that if I swung the bat perfectly, I could ensure that I would get the best candy, but there was always a good chance that I would swing the bat too hard, break the piñata, and be the *last* kid to get the good candy. I used a little bit of strategy and a whole lot of luck, and I swung for the fences knowing I'd either hit a home run or strike out completely. All or nothing. That was my natural play style. Even in my childhood I was the Wild Man.

Why is this my natural playing style? I have no idea. Some kids are born on the Mr. Tight/Aggressive side of the graph, some on the Bully side, and some on the Wild Man side. All I know is, looking back at my life, it's obvious to me that I was naturally oriented toward playing wildly, loosely, and aggressively.

I'd place my natural playing style on the graph somewhere in between the Bully and the Wild Man, leaning more toward the Wild Man. I'd place myself higher than the *total* Wild Man on the strategy side of the graph, since the *total* Wild Man has *no* concept of strategy. As a kid I was very strategy conscious. I just had a tendency, more often than not, to prefer strategies that relied heavily on luck to win—though I always felt like I made my own luck. I also place myself a little bit on the Bully side of the graph since, while I did take big risks, I didn't *only* take big risks; I often relied on my ingenuity and aggressiveness to win, just like the Bully.

Every time I take a reality check, the first thing I do is take a split second to think back to that eight-year-old kid taking that big risk and calculating that perfect swing.

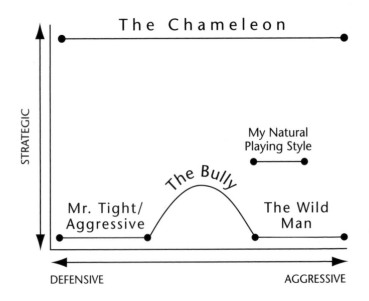

While the answer to question 1—What is your natural style of play?—may never change, in many ways I think it is the most important question of the reality check. We never truly outgrow our natural styles. At best, we learn to control them. Even today, I still have to remind myself that if left unchecked, I will almost always revert to the Wild Man. Not that being the Wild Man is always a bad thing. The flip side to question 1 is that every hour of the day I'm reminded to keep an eye out for situations in which my natural style will come in handy. When those moments arise, I always know I'll be bringing my A-game.

Question 2: How Big Is Your Chip Stack?

When playing in a poker tournament, at least once an hour I'll take a mental chip count of the entire table. I'll compare my stack to those around me and gauge where I stand in the pecking order. Am I the biggest stack? If so, by how much? Am I the smallest stack? Am I in the top three? Do I have a two-to-one chip ratio over anyone else at the table?

If possible, I'll also take a tournament-wide chip count as well. Lots of times there's a leader board that will tell you who has the most chips and what the average stack size is. It's always important to see if you've got more chips than the average stack in the tournament. If you don't, you know it's time to get to work. If there isn't a leader board visible, I'll try and eyeball the tables around me to guesstimate the chip average. How does my chip stack compare to the other tables? If I were suddenly moved to *that* table, how would I compare? Would I still be on top?

At work, taking a chip count is just as easy. Every hour, take a moment to think about your position within the company. Where do you stand in the pecking order? Instead of chips, think in terms of how much leverage you have. Think in terms of how much power you have. While this may seem like little more than a piss-ing contest, question 2 goes a lot deeper than just "Am I beating the other guy?" Actually taking a moment and looking at where you *really* stand in your company can be a rude awakening for some—and a real eye-opener.

Over time, people have a tendency to convince themselves that they are in a better position in their company than they actu-ally are, or vice versa. If every hour of every working day you take a brief moment to think about how your chips stack up in relation to the rest of your company, you'll make sure that you never lose per-spective or delude yourself. Hey, nobody said taking a reality check was easy!

But question 2 doesn't end there. Taking a chip count doesn't only relate to your position within the company—it's important to take a chip count in *every* business situation. Let's say you're in a boardroom meeting attempting to close a big deal. Take a mo-ment and look around the table and take a chip count. Who's in the driver's seat? Who has the big chip stack? Using their leverage and power, who can push the rest of the table around? In a room with four of your colleagues you may be the small stack, but in a meeting with four *different* colleagues you may be the big stack. You wouldn't play the same with a big stack as you would with a small one, would you?

Now, let's take it one step further. What's the chip stack of your company in relation to the rest of your industry? In relation to global business? When meeting with a potential client or even a rival company, you no longer have just *your* personal chip count to calculate; you have to think about your company's chip count as a whole. Is your company the big stack in the industry? Can you bully other companies around? Or do you work for a small stack? Just like in tournament play, you're not only playing your stack against the other stacks at your table, you're also playing your stack against the stacks of the entire tournament.

Taking a moment to think about and even visualize your chip stack can really help you narrow down your playing options, formulate the correct strategy, and ensure that you have a *realistic* view of where you stand at all times.

Question 3: What Are Your Strengths and Weaknesses?

A few years back I headed a small start-up company that made ergonomic laptop accessories. It all began with the LapSaver, a product I created and developed. The LapSaver was a device designed to keep your laptop computer comfortably secure on your lap when you were working away from your desk. After I created the LapSaver and found a partner to take it to market, I became really excited with the idea of creating a whole line of ergonomic laptop products. But before the LapSaver had hit store shelves, I was on to my next product. I trusted the partner would do everything right. After all, it was a reasonably sized business with a line of computer accessories available nationwide in large retail chains. So, I started moving my attention to the next product.

Unfortunately, the partner ended up having financial problems and never got the LapSaver to market, declaring bankruptcy in the process. I tried in vain to bring the LapSaver to market myself, but a crash hit the industry shortly after this time and the nationwide retailers that had been interested in it decreased the number of vendors they worked with, freezing me out. At the end of the day, I had to shut down the company.

Perhaps there is no way I could have ever seen this coming—regardless of the amount of due diligence I performed. The partner was very careful to keep its true financial situation from me. But to this day I wonder if I could have prevented the mistake of choosing the incorrect partner by paying more attention to the details at hand. I'm not sure it would have made any difference to the outcome of the business—the industry slowdown still would have affected us and the LapSaver may still not have been successful in the market-place. But it's still something I think about from time to time.

From this experience I learned that my strengths lie in my abilities as an idea man. My strength is in my vision. I am great at taking a new idea and driving it hard, stretching it as far as it can go, and creating an overall vision for the potential of a company and its products.

My weakness lies in my lack of attention to the details. And you know what they say: the devil's in the details.

Part of what helps ensure I don't repeat the same mistake over and over again is my hourly reality check. By regularly noting my strengths and weaknesses I make sure that I never again fall into the trap of letting the details slip away from me. That's why today I always put extra emphasis on the details of every project I take on. Since I know the idea man side of me will do its thing on its own, I always double up on the details side to compensate. I even go out of my way to hire people on my team who have a great eye for detail. With all of these safety measures in place, no one would ever know that I had a weakness in the details department to begin with.

In short, a person who is aware of their strengths and weaknesses always knows how to best utilize their strengths and compensate for their weaknesses. It's a necessary component of the reality check.

Question 4: What's Your Table Image?

Now that you've taken a good long look at yourself—your natural style, the size of your chip stack, and your strengths and weaknesses—it's important to take a moment to think about how *other* players perceive you.

If I were to sit down at a No-Limit Hold 'Em table and play tightly/aggressively for two hours straight, everyone at that table would assume that I was a tight/aggressive player in general. If I had a big stack in front of me but never put much of it into play, people would assume I was a player who doesn't take many risks, a player who isn't looking to make big moves.

On top of that, a table of total strangers will have a very different view of my playing style than a table full of my friends will. Depending on how you play and who you play against, each person in each situation will have a different read on who you are. Because of this, each person will formulate a different strategy against you. Every one of your actions and decisions form together to create what is called your *table image*.

In all situations it is important to consider your table image. Your boss, who has only been in meetings with you when you've been very quiet, has a very different read on you than do your coworkers with whom you interact every day. Before you can formulate a prudent strategy, you first have to consider what table image your actions have created and whether that table image works *for* you or *against* you.

Your table image doesn't only apply to your daily office life. Just as in question 2 where you visualized our chip stack both in *and* outside the context of your company, it's important to apply the table image concept to all facets of your business life. The company for whom you work has a table image. What actions has your company taken within your industry lately? Has it affected how others will view your company? When you represent your company, it's important to not only represent your company's chip stack, but to represent their table image as well.

Only once you've taken all of this into consideration will you be ready to formulate a proper strategy.

Question 5: What's It Going to Take to Leave Feeling Like a Winner?

This is a hard one to answer. I think you'll find that by asking yourself this question you're not always going to get the obvious answer you'd expect. I always end my reality check by asking myself what it's going to take to leave feeling like a winner because I find it to be the most centering of all the questions. This is the question that puts everything into perspective and reminds me what I'm doing this whole work thing for in the first place.

Not everyone wants or needs to be a CEO. In fact, a very small percentage of us will ever have the opportunity to sit atop a large corporation. Not everyone needs or wants to be making a seven-figure salary every year. While I'm sure most people wouldn't turn down a million bucks if it were handed to them on the street, not everyone wants or needs to work the hours it takes, on average, to earn a yearly seven-figure salary.

When it comes to success, there are no rules. No one in the world can dictate what is going to make you feel successful. Everyone has their own definition of success. The only thing that matters is that you figure out exactly what it's going to take to walk away feeling like a winner. What is it going to take to make you feel like a success? That's the only question you ever have to ask yourself in your career.

The big-picture answer to the question is often a tough one to come up with. Not everyone knows exactly where they want to be one year from now, or ten years from now, and on down the line. Yet, I find that by simply *attempting* to answer the question multiple times each day, I get closer and closer to defining my overall idea of success, and thus closer to understanding how to achieve it.

But the big picture isn't the *whole* picture. While understanding what will make you feel like a success in the future and figuring out how to achieve that success should be your overall career goal, every day you are faced with a handful of situations that you can apply this question to. The reason I ask myself question 5 every hour of every working day is so that I can focus on feeling like a winner and a success in everything I do, big or small.

Even if you don't know what will make you feel like a success when you walk away from your career, I'll bet you can figure out what will make you feel like a success when you walk away from your next meeting. Whenever I go into a meeting I think about what it's going to take to leave that meeting feeling as though I succeeded, feeling as though I accomplished everything I wanted to accomplish and got the most out of the experience as a whole. I apply this question to business lunches, phone calls, interviews, boardroom meetings, and every project or deal that I take on. If feeling like a success means doing the minimal amount of work on a given project so that you can pay more attention to your family, or vice versa, then make peace with that and be aware of it from the get-go. Taking a reality check on what you need to do in every area of your life in order to feel like a success will not only help you sleep at night, it will fill everything you do with purpose and resolve.

Each hour of each working day, end your reality check by making sure you're doing what it takes, in the grand scheme of things as well as in the minutiae of day-to-day living, to walk away feeling like a winner.

THE CHAMELEON'S REALITY CHECK

If you could speed up the reality check by answering all five questions and formulating a strategy in the blink of an eye, you would begin to understand the thought process of the Chameleon. The more often you take a reality check, the faster it will become second nature to you. By doing so, the appropriate strategy for each situation will come to you more quickly and the strategies themselves will become stronger.

While I recommend you take a reality check every hour of every working day, even doing so only once or twice a day can greatly improve your business acumen and your overall gamesmanship. The reality check not only gives you a deeper understanding of yourself and a greater perspective of the company you work for, but it can help you unleash your full potential and realize your goals.

So now that you've taken a reality check and gathered up all of that information, what do you do with it?

You formulate a strategy.

As an example, let's go back to Jim and his fateful first poker tournament—the one that he walked out of with his head held low and his self-esteem dashed—and let's see how a reality check could have improved Jim's chances of winning.

JIM'S REALITY CHECK

Imagine we've just traveled back in time to Jim's first No-Limit Hold 'Em tournament at the exact moment he began losing his chip stack. Jim's just been moved to his second table. He'd quadrupled his chip stack since the tourney began by playing wildly and aggressively. He has a big pile of chips in front of him and he's feeling confident. Everyone at this new table is sizing him up, staring at his chip stack and wondering what kind of a player he is. Since Jim just moved to this table, no one here has any idea what a hot streak he's been on. Jim's going to have no problem pushing this table around, or at least that's what he's thinking. The floor man announces that the first hour is up—no more rebuys allowed. Everyone's got to play with what they've got in front of them. That's fine by Jim—he thinks he's gonna tear up this table.

Let's find out what would happen if Jim had stopped right at that moment and taken a quick reality check.

Question 1: What is Jim's natural playing style?

Well, just like me, Jim has a tendency to play like the Wild Man, which is pretty much how he's been playing so far in this tournament. Playing like the Wild Man hasn't hurt him yet. Because of the rebuy situation, everyone else was playing wildly and aggressively, and since that's Jim's natural style of play, Jim had no problem jumping in and playing along.

On second thought, Jim did get pretty lucky on a few of those hands. Especially the ones he went all in with. Jim would usually never go all in with an A-10 off-suit, but since he knew he could re-buy if he lost the hand, and since Jim believed the guy who bet into him had a worse hand than he, Jim played it. Luckily for Jim, he hit an ace on the flop and a ten on the river, and was able to double up pretty quickly.

Jim's natural playing style is the Wild Man, and so far it's been working. So far.

Question 2: How big is Jim's chip stack?

Right now Jim's got a little over $2,000 in chips sitting in front of him. He started with $500. Not bad. Looking around the table he sees three other players with stacks comparable to his. Although Jim's is definitely the biggest at the table, he's probably only $500 ahead of the other three big stacks. That's not much of a lead. One big chip swing could easily change his position at that table. Two players at the table have small stacks, with only $500 or so in chips. They probably called for a rebuy moments before the first hour was up. The other three players at the table all have somewhere between $800 and $1,200 chips each, putting the average chip stack at Jim's table at around $1,100. Jim's stack is about $900 chips over the average. That's good, but not great.

Having checked his table out, Jim takes a further glance around the room. There's no leader board, so he has to visually eyeball the other tables. At the table closest to Jim's there is another player who looks to have around $2,000 in chips sitting in front of him. As a whole, the rest of his table is doing better than Jim's table. Nobody seems to have less than $1,000 in chips in front of them. The average stack size for that table is around $1,400. If Jim were at that table he'd have only $600 more than the average chip stack. That's not a very big lead.

Jim glances at the only other table he can get a good look at. The average stack at that table looks to be about the same as at his table, although, from what he can see, the biggest stack looks to be around $1,500.

Jim places the average chip stack for the entire tournament at around $1,200. He's not sure if he's the biggest stack in the tournament, since he can't see all the tables, but he's definitely up there. Jim's lead isn't as big as he had imagined when he first sat down at this table, considering there's only around $800 of chips between Jim and the average stack in the tournament. The upside is that it looks as though Jim's table has a slightly lower chip stack average than some of the other tables, giving him an advantage over the big stacks at the other tables. The downside is that, overall in the tournament, Jim's chip lead isn't very impressive.

Question 3: What are Jim's strengths and weaknesses?

Jim's strengths in poker lie in his ability to see the potential of a given situation and to maximize that potential whenever possible. Jim has always had an innate ability to calculate the potential worth of a given hand in relation to the players he's playing against, and squeeze that hand for every dime possible. The moment he gets a good hand and a good flop he takes stock of who is entering the pot with him and quickly figures out what size bet is going to keep them in the hand and what size bet is going to scare them away. I'm not sure how Jim does this, but he does it against me all the time when we play together. As a poker player it's definitely his greatest strength.

Jim's weakness lies in the fact that he can often get caught up in winning and rush himself to death. He gets emotionally caught up in the game and can quickly lose a few hands due to careless playing.

Since Jim has just come off of a big win, and because of this reality check he knows he has a tendency to get caught up in rushing, Jim understands he needs to cool down a bit before he make any more big plays. By taking the reality check Jim has also reminded himself of one of his poker strengths and will keep an eye open for an opportunity to utilize it.

Question 4: What's Jim's table image?

Since Jim just moved to this table and no one there has ever played with him before, he doesn't have much of a table image at all. What he does have is a big chip stack in front of him, which can often speak louder than actions. Everyone here either thinks Jim's been getting really lucky or that he knows what he's doing—either way, no one is dying to get into a pot with him. It's the small stacks that everyone is gunning for.

While no one at the table has an idea of Jim's playing style, there were a handful of people who played with him at the first table and also survived the first hour. If Jim is moved to another table later on in the tournament and comes face to face with any of them again, they'll remember him as a wild, loose player. That holds no bearing at the moment, but it's something to keep in mind.

Basically, Jim's a clean slate at this new table—a clean slate with a big stack. While everyone would like to take this stack away from Jim, they're all going to be a bit timid betting into him, knowing that he can call a lot of bets without blinking an eye.

Question 5: What's it going to take for Jim to leave feeling like a winner?
Since this is the first tournament Jim has ever played in, he doesn't feel a great pressure to finish high in the rankings. Although taking home first place and walking out with that big cash prize would be great, Jim can't expect to win on his very first endeavor. So the big question is: What is it going to take for Jim to leave feeling as though he played to his best abilities? What's it going to take for Jim to leave feeling like a success?

Jim takes a moment, thinks it over, and decides that his goal isn't to make it to the final table or even to finish in the money. Jim's goal is to finish in the top 50 percent of the field; to not make any careless, rookie mistakes; and to walk away a better player than he was when he sat down.

Now that Jim has asked himself all five of the reality check questions, what has he learned?

He's learned that he needs to pull back his natural playing style and tone down the Wild Man within. He's learned that while his chip stack may be large, it's no reason to feel overly confident.

He's reminded himself of his strengths and weaknesses, and to keep a watchful eye out for both. He's also learned that his table image, at this point in the tournament, is what he makes of it. Finally, Jim has learned that if he places in the top 50 percent and doesn't make any big mistakes, he will leave feeling like a success.

While I can't travel back in time and tell you what would have happened differently in this tournament if Jim had given himself a reality check (although I'm sure Jim wishes I could), I can guarantee you that by simply taking that moment to slow down and think about his game plan he would have been able to formulate a better strategy. At the least, Jim would have tightened up his play and focused on creating an advantageous table image. Those two simple tasks alone would have kept Jim around in the tournament a few hours longer than he lasted without them.

One thing I know for sure: If Jim had taken a quick reality check, he wouldn't have walked out of that tournament with a head filled with *if only* thoughts. That alone is priceless.

By taking a reality check, understanding your strengths and weaknesses, and then figuring out the best strategy to employ in each situation, you'll be well on your way to being a great, agile competitor. You'll be on your way to becoming the Chameleon.

It took me many, many years and a lot of mistakes to learn that in order to succeed in this world you have to be brave enough to take a good, long look at yourself. You have to be real with yourself to understand exactly what it is you can add to this world and what it is that you can take away.

My strengths have always been in my passion and in my vision. While I am able to use those strengths as leverage, I know that I will need to have the full package to be able to move ahead in my career. I have to be more than just my combined strengths. An hourly reality check helps me stretch beyond my potential and gets me closer and closer to my goals, each hour of every day.

One day I might decide that I'd rather be an inventor or some other occupation that relies purely on passion and vision, but for right now I'm focused on becoming a Chameleon. It's the only way I can imagine feeling successful. Like I said before, the only question each one of us ever has to answer in our lives is: *What is it going to take to walk away feeling like a winner?*

....

THE SHOWDOWN

Take an hourly reality check in order to stay sharp and aware at all times. Know yourself in order to unleash your true potential.

....

LEAVE YOUR EMOTIONS AT THE DOOR
Going on Tilt

There will never be a *definitive guide* to business or poker. There are simply too many scenarios and too many factors to take into consideration for one book to ever give you the correct answer for every possible situation. While someone may be able to give you the answer for how to play two certain cards against a certain flop at a certain blind level, that same answer could very well become incorrect depending on the players you are playing against or even the stage of the tournament you are in. The best path to improving either your business or your poker game is to become familiar with the most common situations you will come across and to learn the questions you can ask yourself that will help you make the best decisions in each of those situations.

There are no right answers. The key is to learn the right questions to ask yourself.

Chapters 1 through 3 served as the foundation for applying poker strategy to your business life. I've covered the basics of both games. You now know what to look out for in your opponents, you know how to combat almost every playing style you're liable to come across (or at the least an iteration of that style), and you've learned the process by which you can become a better, more conscious player. The next seven chapters will pose the most common—and the most important—situations you're liable to come across both in business and in poker. Now you're getting to the *meat* of the book.

The next seven chapters will be concerned with practical applications for business and poker strategy as well as a few tricks of the trade that will help you win often, and win big.

Since this is the first situational chapter, we'll start with a situation every player likes the least. Let's get it out of the way, if you will. This is a situation that every player, especially the beginner, often comes across. In fact, it's probably the most common situation (or maybe tied for the most common situation—if you're lucky) that players deal with throughout their lives. It's a situation that no one looks forward to, that every player wants to avoid, but that everyone must face at least once every time they sit down at a poker table, and more than a handful of times throughout their business career. What situation is that, you ask?

Losing.

Everyone loses. It's something you simply can't avoid. The best players in the world lose—often, in fact. While the professional poker player and the corporate CEO may lose *less often* than the rest of us, they still lose a good deal of the time as well. So, since everyone loses, it's obviously not the *act of losing* that's the problem, it's *how you lose*. The difference between a good player and a bad player is that the good player can take a loss and come back swinging, while the bad player lets the loss put him on tilt—and then he loses everything.

This chapter is about how to lose in the most effective way possible. It's about damage control. After all, taking a loss is fine— it's expected. But taking a loss that causes you to play below your skill level, or possibly even lose all your chips because of it, is *never* fine. This chapter is about taking a loss and learning how to prevent yourself from going on tilt.

FRIENDS DON'T LET FRIENDS GO ON TILT

In discussing the Wild Man in chapter 2 I briefly touched upon the concept of going on tilt. While the Wild Man may be the most prone to going on tilt of the three player types, going on tilt definitely isn't a trait exclusive to Wild Men. To lose and to get upset is a natural human trait, but that doesn't mean it has to be impossible to control. In fact, learning to control your losses and come back swinging is a trait any player, in business or in poker, should be able to master quickly and easily.

In pinball, when a player gets frustrated and tries to cheat by physically bumping or tilting the machine to help move the pinball around, it causes a mechanism in the machine to lock up and the game to automatically end. No matter how high your score is, if you bump the machine hard enough to trigger the sensor, the machine will freeze up and shut down, and a flashing light will go off while the word TILT blinks mockingly in your face. Game over.

I'm not sure who the first person was to transplant this phrase from the arcade to the poker room, but the phrase fits like a glove. In poker, when the game is not going in the direction a player wants it to, or if that player has just taken a big loss, out of sheer frustration that player may try to get the game to do something it's not supposed to do, such as pay off with bad or mediocre cards, thus causing the game to freeze up and end suddenly for that player. While a blinking light and the word TILT may not flash above the poker table, I guarantee you that any player who's ever lost all his chips from going on tilt will agree: *you see that damn blinking light.*

HOW BAD BEATS LEAD TO GOING ON TILT

The most common cause of an "on tilt" meltdown is a bad beat. The first step to learning how to handle a loss and to prevent going on tilt is to learn how to handle a bad beat. Bad beats are the hands that, statistically, you should have won. They are the hands in which you were the favorite to win, but lost instead. Usually, a bad

THE FLOP

YOU   OPPONENT

A great flop for you. So far, so good.

beat ends with your opponent outdrawing you on the river, known as "sucking out" on the river, with a card that was something like a one-in-twenty shot to appear on the board.

Let's say you enter the pot with big slick (common poker slang for A-K) and the flop comes: seven, king, four. You've got top pair, a pair of kings, with top kicker, the ace. You're a definite favorite in this hand. You make a decent-sized bet and you get called. Next card comes: an ace. You've got top two pair, aces and kings—practically the nuts. All you've got to worry about is your opponent having trips (three of a kind), with either pocket aces, sevens, or fours. It's always possible, but you've got top two pairs and a very good shot at winning the pot. If the other guy has got you beat with trips, then he's got you beat, but you're ready to go down with this hand if need be.

Since you want to find out right there and then where the other player stands, you put him all in. He thinks about it for a minute—

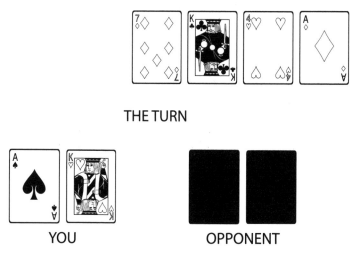

THE TURN

YOU   **OPPONENT**

Things are even better for you on the turn. This hand should be in the bag.

a good sign for you—and then calls. He turns over pocket queens. He called you with *pocket queens*? With an ace and a king showing on the board? Is this guy crazy? You smile gleefully and start picturing what all of his chips are going to look like piled up in front of you. You turn over your cards and show him top two pairs. Aces and kings, sucker. He doesn't even flinch. Dealer turns the river card.

You've got to be kidding me.

Wouldn't you know it: *a queen*. He hits trips on fifth street and pulls out a long-shot win. There were only two cards in the whole deck that could have helped him, and one of them just broke your heart.

That's a bad beat.

That's the type of hand you wish you could rewind and play again. It's the type of hand that will leave you stewing at the table for the next few minutes, replaying it in your mind over and over again.

How could I have lost? I was the winner! Damn it, I had that hand! Those chips should be in front of me!

Suffering a bad beat will put your emotional strength to the test. If you let the bad beat consume you with thoughts like *"That's not fair!"* and *"I'm gonna get that guy!"* then you've let the situation take control of you. That's when you go on tilt. For the next few hands you play anything with a picture card. You bet big. You try to push the rest of the table around. You want your money back, damn it! You feel you deserve to win a hand.

Just let me win a hand! I should be winning!

But you don't win. Instead, you end up reducing your chip stack to the point where you have to go all in with an Alamo hand—a last-stand hand that you have no choice but to play because of the size of the blinds—and you lose all of your money.

You walk out of the casino, or your friend's living room, in a total state of shock.

What just happened in there? How stupid am I?

It works the same way in the business world.

We've all seen it happen. Some guy in a meeting will get a major project pulled out from under him, or a major promotion he thought he was in line for will get passed on to someone else. He'll think he has to speak up and say his piece on the subject right then and there in the company- or group-wide meeting. The boss barely knows this guy's name but here he is at a meeting, shouting and ranting. Meanwhile all of his coworkers are hiding their faces in embarrassment, mouthing "You've got to be kidding me" to one another while rolling their eyes. The boss humors this guy and does his best to curtail him and move on to real issues, but this guy just won't give it up. He makes a total fool of himself.

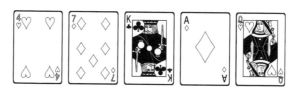

THE RIVER

YOU   OPPONENT

Ouch! That's what we call a bad beat.

Back in his office this guy rapidly fires a few dozen flaming e-mails to everyone at the company, *including the boss*, explaining his actions in further detail and pleading for understanding and recognition. In the hopes of saving their coworker any further embarrassment, his e-mails go completely ignored by everyone. Frustrated, he complains to his coworkers who, at this point, don't even know what to say to him. Nobody wants to get dragged down alongside this guy. He's spiraling out of control.

In his quintessential moment of hitting rock bottom, he decides he needs to take this up directly with his boss, get it off his chest for good and explain himself to the only person who will understand—the man on top. He storms off toward the boss's office—and toward his inevitable self-destruction. He's gone way too far. He has no idea what he's doing. He's lost perspective and control. He's completely on tilt.

When you go on tilt, you lose all recognition of what you're doing. It's like you're intoxicated with anger and regret. You're in a dangerous situation and you continue to let it get worse, moment by moment. It's like creating your own private perfect storm.

In poker it all happens so quickly, in contrast to business, where going on tilt can stretch out for longer periods. Everything in poker is magnified and sped up. When you go on tilt in poker, you can go from big stack to small stack to no stack in a matter of just a few hands. When you go on tilt in the business world, it can take place over a period of a few days, a few weeks, or longer. It's often harder to spot if you're on tilt in the business world because you can become so accustomed to acting irrationally over a period of time that you forget you were ever put on tilt in the first place.

Relationships are everything in business. A bad day, or a bad beat, can cause you to act rashly and say the wrong thing to a colleague, your boss, or even a potential client. You can easily lose your composure and lash out. By doing so you break that trust and betray the table image you've worked so hard to create at your company or in your industry. Whether it's a coworker or your boss, once you've allowed yourself to go on tilt and you've broken that trust, it's going to be very hard to win it back. Knowing that you've crossed a line with that person, you begin acting as you would never normally act toward them, out of either fear or resentment. You exacerbate the situation, and it snowballs into a completely dysfunctional working relationship. From one small moment in which you allowed yourself to go on tilt you've done what very well could be irreparable damage to a business relationship.

So how can you stop yourself from letting a bad beat cause you to go on tilt? The first step is in recognizing the situations that put you on tilt, bad beats or otherwise, *as they're happening.*

HOW TO KNOW WHEN YOU'RE ABOUT TO GO ON TILT

How can you recognize when you're about to go on tilt? If you know what kind of personality you are, what your player type is, you'll be able to recognize what situations have the potential of putting you on tilt. Everyone gets angry. Everyone gets upset. Some people are just better at dealing with it than others. To be successful in business or poker, you have to be able to control yourself emotionally. You just *have to.*

But it's not only bad beats that can put you on tilt. Sometimes it's the actions of another player that can cause you to lose your focus and control. The simple act of watching another player win a ton of chips while you haven't won any at all can cause you to go on tilt. Because of resentment and jealousy, you may start playing worse against that player. You may want to show him up. You may want to see him lose. The problem is that he's got you just where he wants you now because you're playing without thinking. You're playing emotionally, and unless luck is on your side, you're going to end up giving away all of your chips—or the equivalent in the business world: you end up getting fired.

Personally, when I hear that someone has been saying something negative about me behind my back, or spreading information about me that isn't true, it can really tick me off. If left unchecked, something like that can cause me to go on tilt. Watching someone who is basically always managing up—meaning they're working only for the attention of their superiors and never for the good of the team or the company—can also get me very fired up and potentially put me off my game.

We all have a concept of fairness in our minds, and when reality fails to live up to our standard of what is fair and what is not, it can upset us and cause us to think or act irrationally. We're all human. If a person who I don't think has the company's best interest in mind gets a big budget approved for his or her team—a budget that my team could have put to much better use—I will feel as though I've been treated unfairly. But what am I going to do about it? Am I going to complain to my boss? No, because it would just end up looking like sour grapes. There's nothing I can do. The key is to accept that my preconceived notion of fairness doesn't amount to jack squat in the reality of the business world or the poker table. All I can do is make sure I'm taking extra care that I don't act on those emotions, that I don't end up lashing out at someone and putting my position with the company in jeopardy.

It's not just bad beats and other players that can put me on tilt; I can put *myself* on tilt. I know that if I don't get enough sleep I can get irritable and easily angered, and when I get angry I can be very difficult to deal with. Sometimes that can be the difference between closing a deal and not closing a deal. If I come into work without having slept enough and someone tells me something I don't want to hear—I don't care if it's the CEO himself—I know I have the potential in those situations to say something I'm going to regret. In those situations I'm not my normal self.

Those are a few of the situations that can put me on tilt. What situations put you on tilt? Take a moment and think of what scenarios and factors could lead to losing control and going on tilt at work or at the poker table. Obviously, everyone hates losing a big hand or getting passed up for a big promotion, but if you can pinpoint the little things, whether it's not getting enough sleep or watching bad players win lucky pots, you'll always know when you have the potential to go on tilt.

To truly understand what sets you on tilt, it's important to boil it down to its simplest terms. At its essence, what is it that puts you on tilt? For me, and probably for most people, I go on tilt when I get too angry. Something ticks me off, my frustration level gets out of control, and I lose focus. Some people go on tilt in completely the opposite way: they become overly introverted or quiet. Whether out of fear or embarrassment, they shut down and clam up. At the poker table, when this type of player goes on tilt he tightens up his play beyond reason, so afraid of taking any more bad beats and losing any more of his chips.

Usually—not always—but usually, your natural style will have a direct correlation with the way you go on tilt. Players closer to the Wild Man side of the graph tend to go on tilt by getting too angry. Players on the Mr. Tight/Aggressive side of the graph tend to become overly passive when they go on tilt. Understanding your natural playing style, as discussed in rule 3, can help you recognize what type of on-tilt player you are, and better prepare you for preventing those situations from getting out of control. Do you tighten up your hands or do you loosen up your hands when you go on tilt?

The first step you can take in preventing yourself from going on tilt is to be aware of what situations have the potential to put you on tilt and to always keep a watchful eye out for those situations. Bottom line: always be prepared to go on tilt.

HOW TO STOP YOURSELF FROM GOING ON TILT

If you're always prepared in case you go on tilt, you'll never be surprised when it's about to happen. Next time you push a lot of chips into the middle of the table on a big hand, before the final showdown, tell yourself that there's a chance you may lose this hand. Don't jinx yourself or think negatively, but just remind yourself that it's a game and that sometimes you're going to lose. Even better, every time you push some chips into the middle, remind yourself that there's always a certain amount of luck involved in every hand of poker and that losing this hand is no reason to get upset and play stupidly. Being prepared to go on tilt is the first step in preventing on tilt situations.

The second step is to *let it go*. The minute you put your chips in the middle, you've given them away. If you win the hand, they're yours again, but every time you put chips into a pot, be okay with letting those chips go permanently. After all, if you don't think you have a good chance at winning the pot you shouldn't be playing in the first place. But unless you've got the absolute nuts, there's always a chance you're going to lose. The minute you put chips in the pot, the minute you take a chance on a big deal, let go of whatever you've put into the pot and make peace with it. In business, every time you put your neck on the line or get your hopes up about a deal or a promotion, be prepared for things not to work out in your favor. Make peace with that and remind yourself that some things in life are simply out of your control.

If the beat was so bad, or the loss so heavy, that you feel you're about to go on tilt and can't calm yourself down to save your life, the best advice—as obvious as it may sound—is to take a walk. Whether you take a walk around your office or around the poker room, just get up and move around. *Walk it off*. Regroup yourself, assess the situation, and don't allow yourself to play again until you've completely calmed down. Allow yourself the time to calm down before you make any further decisions. As I said earlier, everyone gets upset—it's what you do when you're upset that matters. Also, don't get even more upset at yourself for getting upset in the first place. It's normal. Congratulate yourself for recognizing that you were about to go on tilt and prevented yourself from acting on those emotions.

To stop yourself from going on tilt in business and poker:

♣ Always be prepared to go on tilt.

♣ Every time you put chips into the pot, let them go.

♣ If you still feel yourself going on tilt, take a walk and calm yourself down before you make any further decisions.

The measure of a great player is not how many big pots he wins or how many big deals he closes, but how many big losses he is able to recover from and come back a winner. Everyone struggles with going on tilt. The best poker players in the world and the biggest CEOs still have to work to control themselves emotionally. If you didn't get emotionally involved in the game, it wouldn't be worth playing. Being able to rein yourself in is just another muscle to exercise in order to get stronger, same as any other skill you develop in order to improve your game.

Not to extend the metaphor too far, but outside of poker and business, one of my other passions in life is skiing. Whenever someone learns how to ski, the first thing an instructor teaches him is how to stop. The only way to learn how to ski is to have the confidence to pick up a little speed on the slopes. If you're not going fast enough, you won't be able to turn, and if you can't turn, you're probably going to fall. But if you learn how to comfortably come to a full stop, you won't be afraid of picking up a little speed.

In poker and in business, if you learn how to stop yourself, to slow down and gain control, you'll have earned the right to play a little faster and take a few more chances. Put simply: you'll be able to have a lot more fun.

....

THE SHOWDOWN

Whether you're at a poker table or a boardroom meeting—NEVER lose control of your emotions.

....

MAKE THE MOST OUT OF A GREAT HAND
Slow-Playing

So, you've finally landed a great hand. The dealer just turned the first three community cards and showed you exactly what you wanted to see. Sure, you've stolen a few blinds throughout the night, taken down a few medium-sized pots here and there, even made a gut-shot straight to win a hand you shouldn't have been playing in the first place, but now you've got the hand you've been waiting for all night. On top of that, you've got a couple of live ones in the hand with you and you're eyeing their chips, thinking how much better they're going to look sitting in front of you. All you have to do is play the rest of the hand just right and you'll get them pushing their chips to the middle, no questions asked. These are the hands you play poker for.

So how are you going to play it?

Y ou've just mapped out a revolutionary business plan. You've worked hard at your job, put in overtime hours, paid your dues, and now you've planned out an idea that has the potential of changing the very way your company does business. On top of that, you have the connections and the experience to take your vision and make it a reality. No one at your company has ever had the vision to branch the company out in this particular direction. It's a completely new idea. It could be the future of your company. All you have to do now is get your company behind the idea. If you play your cards right, you could end up in a VP seat. In fact, they may have to create an entirely new division of the company for you to run. These are the types of moments that only come around a few times in a career.

So how are you going to play it?

I n this chapter we're going to discuss a concept that is widely used in business and poker, but often misunderstood. The concept is slow-playing. At its core, slow-playing means to play weak when you're actually strong. While the full meaning and usage of the concept has many subtleties and nuances, in poker it usually means to check your cards, as opposed to betting them, so as to withhold the true strength of your hand. It can also be used to allow other players to make a second best hand to your best hand. In business it usually means to act in such a way so as to make your opponents believe a particular deal or project is more advantageous or important to them than it is to you. It can also mean to literally slow down by only revealing the necessary pieces of your plan so as to retain control over the situation and keep the rest of the playing field in the dark. Don't worry if some of these concepts sound complicated now; we'll cover all of them in this chapter.

Basically, slow-playing is a way of lulling an opponent into a false sense of security. At least that's how most people understand and utilize slow-playing in their careers and at the poker table. I'm here to tell you that, while slow-playing is a necessary component for all true players to understand and to master, it is rarely advantageous and often riskier than it is beneficial—yet people do it all the time.

There are many reasons people decide to slow-play. In fact, most beginners slow-play like it's going out of style. Slow-playing is a well-known poker concept and it's easy to understand: play weak when you're strong. It's poker strategy 101. You see it in a player's body language when he shakes his head in frustration or when he looks at his cards and says something like, "I really shouldn't be playing this, but what the hell, let's gamble," all the while holding a strong hand. But checking a strong hand and allowing other players a free card is very different from trying to psych out your opponents with body language. In fact, more often than not, checking a strong hand is the wrong move.

I can't count the number of times I've watched some sad sap lose all of his chips by slow-playing pocket aces. I can't fault him—we've all done it. You look down at your cards to find two aces glaring back at you and that little voice in your head says, "Nobody here knows I've got pocket aces; I'm going to lure them all in!" When it's your turn to act, you put on your best poker face and simply check it through. The flop comes three low cards and no one is betting. "Shoot," you think to yourself, "I want to make some money on these aces; I'm going to check and hope someone picks up a decent hand." So you check again, giving a player a free card, and on fourth street you get someone betting into you. "Finally," you think, "these aces are gonna pay off." You reraise and suddenly the guy raises you back. You call because for some reason you've convinced yourself that pocket aces are invincible and you end up losing a big pot on the river to a hand you never saw coming, such as two pair, three of a kind, or even a small straight. If only you had bet those aces on the flop you wouldn't have won a big pot, but you sure wouldn't have lost one either.

Because slow-playing is so commonly used in both business and poker, and because so many people misunderstand it and utilize it incorrectly, it's very important for every player to understand the ins and outs of slow-playing, not only so you can use it correctly yourself but, more importantly, so you can understand how it is so often misused, and how you can use that to your advantage. In this chapter we'll cover the purpose of slow-playing, the right way and the wrong way to slow-play, and the many dangers and pitfalls that come along with it.

WHEN TO SLOW-PLAY IN POKER

By slow-playing you are withholding the true strength of your hand. The purpose of withholding the strength of your hand is to win more money on later betting rounds by allowing your opponent's hand to improve to the point where he or she will bet against you. If you allow your opponent's hand to improve beyond the strength of your hand, you have made a critical mistake. Slow-playing is effective only if you win more money by checking than you would have won by betting. The occasions when it is right to slow-play are very specific and pretty rare.

You should be slow-playing only if *all three* of the following principles apply to your hand:

1. **You've got a very strong hand.** Your hand is so strong that the chance of your opponents catching a hand better than yours is *extremely* small.

2. **You believe a free card will give your opponent the second best hand.** For example, if you flop the ace-high flush and you believe your opponent is on a king-high flush draw, it is often the correct play to slow-play and allow that player a free card in the hopes that he or she will make the second best possible hand, which in that case would be the king-high flush.

3. **The pot is not large.** This is the obvious one. If you've got a very strong hand and there's already a lot of money in the pot, do whatever it takes to win that pot right then and there. It is correct to slow-play only when the pot is small since you are hoping to make the pot larger (yet only so long as you don't jeopardize losing the hand by doing so). Once the pot is nice and big, make a large bet and take it down immediately. Never give your opponents the incentive to call your bet because the pot is big and they have a chance—however small it may be—to win the pot (this is called *pot odds*). Put bluntly: being greedy will more often than not bite you in the ass.

Take some time and look over those three points. You should be slow-playing only in situations when *all three* of those points can be applied to your hand. By slow-playing in any other situation you are taking an unnecessary risk and putting your chip stack in danger. I'll give you one more example of a situation in which slow-playing is the correct play.

Let's say you flop a full house (for example, you have K-9, and the flop comes K, 9, 9) and there's a possible flush draw on the table. Preflop, everyone either limped into the pot or called a small raise, so the pot is still small. You're first to act, so you check it. One of your opponents makes a medium-sized bet and everyone else folds. You simply call the bet here and hope your opponent makes his flush with another flush card on fourth street. If your opponent bets, the correct play is to call. If your opponent checks on the turn and there seems to be little to no chance of his beating your full house, you should check as well and hope his hand improves on the river. While there is a chance your opponent has pocket kings and will beat your full house, it's a very small chance, and you're still correct in slow-playing this hand.

If you're first to act on the river, you have no choice but to bet. You're hoping for a reraise here, because you want your opponent to put as much of his chips into the pot as possible. Because you represented a weak hand, because the pot was small enough at the beginning to warrant slow-playing, and because you believed there was a good chance that your opponent would make a second best hand, slow-playing was the correct play and would most likely win you a big pot in this situation. Remember, slow-play only if you believe that by checking you will make *more* money later on in the hand than if you bet it right there and then.

Once again, if all three slow-playing points are not met, it is incorrect to slow-play.

WHEN TO SLOW-PLAY IN BUSINESS

In business, slow-playing is much easier to pull off and actually a lot safer than it is at the poker table. In fact, almost every business deal involves some form of slow-playing. The very process of negotiating—playing your cards close to your chest, strategically showing only certain components of your hand at certain times—is a form of slow-playing in and of itself. After all, nobody wants to play against aces. If you come into a meeting with the business equivalent of pocket aces, you have to downplay your strength in order to imply a level playing field. It's business 101, but it's also the most effective way of negotiating.

In poker, slow-playing is a tactic rarely used and advantageous only in very specific situations, yet in business slow-playing is probably something you're going to be utilizing—in one form or another—every single day. While we're not going to cover how to slow-play in negotiations and meetings (since it's pretty obvious and I said basically all there is to say on the subject just a few sentences ago), we'll spend the majority of this section covering a lesser known, yet more advantageous, use of the business slow-play: the *long-term* slow-play.

THE LONG-TERM SLOW-PLAY

When you have an idea, product, or project you feel has serious potential, but you're in a company or an industry where big ideas can easily fall by the wayside or be stolen away from you, it is correct to slow-play. You can't come out guns a-blazing with your idea, but you also don't want look like you are trying to deceive your boss or pull a fast one on the company. After all, slow-playing in poker is basically a trick used to deceive your opponents. In business, if you get caught trying to deceive your opponent—especially if that "opponent" is your boss—it's not going to bode well for your future with the company. In business, the correct use of the slow-play isn't about tricking anyone; it's about gathering full strength before you take your idea out to the world. Let me give you an example of a well-executed long-term slow-play.

You've come up with a brand new product that takes advantage of, and stretches across, two separate divisions of your company. You believe it to be the future of your industry. If you were to simply write up a memo to your boss detailing your product and its market potential, the higher-ups would most likely be overwhelmed by the details, bogged down by the numbers, and completely miss your vision and the potential of your idea. Quickly pitching the whole idea to the company benefits no one. And if the company loves it, most likely they'll give leadership of the product over to someone who is already in management of one of the divisions. Not only does this take you out of the picture, but it takes the product out of the hands of the person who knows it best: *you*.

You feel you're the best person to take this product to market, you feel you're the only one with the passion and the vision to see it through. You don't want to just hand it off to your boss and watch it either fall by the wayside or get passed along to someone else. You want to retain control of your idea as long as possible while still keeping the company's best interest in mind. Obviously, if someone else at your company could handle the product better than you, you would have no problem handing it over to them, but since you believe you're the best to bring it to market, you are going to prove it. Instead of just laying your cards on the table, you decide to slow-play it a bit.

Slow-playing at work isn't about being deceptive; it's about being careful how you present an idea. It's about being patient and waiting for the right moment to reveal your hand. It's about putting your best foot forward whenever your neck is on the line.

You take the time to formulate a plan that will allow your product to see the light of day. The first step of your plan is to find the right person to help you introduce your plan to the higher-ups, someone who has ins at the top and will be helpful in getting your product the audience it deserves. Much like when you're slow-playing in poker, you want to make sure you slow-play with the right person. You only want to slow-play in poker against a player you believe has the second best hand. In business, you can't just call up the CEO and pitch your idea, so you find the second best hand equivalent in your company.

You find someone who is willing to take a chance on a new idea, someone who's not afraid of a product with a lot of stretch. You find someone who sees your vision. You lay your whole plan out on the table for this person, you show this person your whole hand—after all, this is the person who is going to be representing you when this idea is brought forth to the brass. There can be no secrets between the two of you. This person is your partner in the slow-play.

You work with this person to create a step-by-step presentation explaining how your product will be realized. You don't need to drop the whole product and all of its far-reaching goals on your company right away; you plan to reveal pieces of it slowly, so as not to overwhelm anyone or make anyone skittish. Sometimes new ideas have the potential of threatening people in higher positions; therefore, you've got to make your idea feel safe to them. You've got to make it clear that you're not looking to steal anyone's job, but to create new value for the company.

You create for yourself a two-year plan or a four-year plan—

whatever would best serve your product. Then you let your slow-play partner, who has the ear of the higher-ups, help take your idea to the right people at the right time. If you've taken the time to correctly choose the best person to champion your idea, then you'll be in good hands as your slow-play partner makes sure that you are able to have your idea heard by the right people.

Finally, once all the pieces are in place, you go in for the win. You've laid the groundwork in your division and, with the help of your slow-play partner, your vision has been pre-sold to the executives, and now they ask you to present your plan to them. Here is your chance to win the big pot and walk away with your dream — leading a new group for the company around your product concept.

The most important factor to remember is that you must play it slowly, taking advantage of all the pieces of the puzzle, getting everyone involved one person at a time. If you rush a great idea you'll never get it to pay off fully. Therefore, you never dump the whole scope of the idea on anyone, instead you let your product unravel slowly over a long period.

If you simply pitched this idea freely to anyone who would listen, you would risk losing the project altogether. Just like in poker, you don't want to bet too big with a strong hand in a small pot and end up winning nothing but the ante. You can't reveal your hand too early in business, either, or you'll only reap the smallest reward. In business, taking down the big pot is taking down a win for both you *and* your company. And when you help your company win, that's when promotions, raises, and bonuses begin to come your way.

A recent example of a different kind of successful long-term slow-play in the business world can be found in Oracle Corporation's acquisition of PeopleSoft Inc. Two of the largest business software developers in the world, Oracle and PeopleSoft began their somewhat friendly merger discussions in 2002, both agreeing that a merge between the two software giants would be beneficial both for the customer and for the industry. When PeopleSoft CEO Craig Conway insisted on remaining the head of the two merged companies, Oracle CEO Larry Ellison balked at the idea, and things quickly turned nasty.

Oracle, dead set on acquiring PeopleSoft, slowly raised its bid over the next three years, but Craig Conway, a former Oracle employee, spearheaded the antimerger campaign against Oracle and seemed equally dead-set on doing whatever he could to prevent the merger. Ellison never raised his acquisition price too quickly, instead raising it in small increments, essentially slow-playing Conway over the next three years. Each time Ellison raised his bid, Conway turned him down, but this didn't cause Ellison to come over the top with a giant bid and try to seal the deal right away. Instead, Ellison had faith that if he waited it out, in time he would get PeopleSoft for a fair price.

Ellison's break came in 2004 when PeopleSoft fired CEO Craig Conway, citing a loss of confidence, and hired back their original CEO, Dave Duffield. With Conway out of the way, Oracle and PeopleSoft were able to return to negotiations. Ellison offered a 10 percent increase in Oracle's all-cash offer, and PeopleSoft agreed to the deal in late 2004 for $10.3 billion.

If Ellison had raised his price too quickly against Conway, there would have been no way he could have gotten PeopleSoft for the fair price he did once Conway had been fired. By taking his time, playing his hand patiently, and waiting for the game to turn in his favor, Larry Ellison successfully closed the deal on one of the largest software mergers in business history, and he did it with a successful long-term slow-play.

Y ou've seen examples of a correct slow-play in poker and in business. Now let's take a look at the many incorrect ways of slow-playing, and how you can take advantage of these mistakes when opponents make them against you.

THE DANGERS OF SLOW-PLAYING

The most obvious danger of slow-playing in poker is that you can allow your opponent to improve his hand beyond the strength of your hand. By checking and allowing your opponent a free card, or even two free cards, you leave yourself open to losing to a hand your opponent would have folded had you bet in a previous betting round.

You also risk slow-playing against someone who is slow-playing *you*. Let's say you have the complete nuts and decide to slow-play, but your opponent has an extremely strong hand as well. Your opponent would never assume you have the complete nuts; therefore, he believes his hand to be stronger. By slow-playing against a player who believes he has the stronger hand, you lose out on opportunities to bet and increase the pot size. That's why slow-playing with the complete nuts isn't usually the correct play. When you have a hand locked up—meaning there's no possible hand that can beat you—you're better off betting and hoping your opponent has a strong hand. In those situations, because your hand is so strong, your best bet is to play it straight up, betting aggressively and hoping your opponent has a strong enough hand to call you.

Allowing your opponents to have good pot odds is also a danger in slow-playing. If you let the pot get large enough to warrant a call by a player who is on a draw, you have made a mistake. Let's say your opponent has a ten-to-one shot that the card he needs will appear on the river—a card that will give him the stronger hand. As long as the amount of money he has to put in the pot in order to call your bet is greater than a ten-to-one ratio in comparison to the total pot size, you have allowed that opponent to make a correct call.

The math gets a little complicated here, and I don't want to get bogged down in game theory, statistics, or probabilities, but here's a crash course in pot odds. If there's a large pot, and the size of the bet your opponent has to call in order to see the next card is small enough that he thinks it's worth a gamble, you have made a mistake in slow-playing this hand. Anytime you allow your opponent to make a *correct* decision, you put your chips in danger. Of course, if you followed the three slow-playing principles, you would never have slow-played a large pot in the first place and therefore would never have found yourself in that situation.

Since so many players overutilize slow-playing, it's easy to take advantage of their mistakes. Think of slow-playing as a very obvious tell. The next time a player checks to you throughout a hand or quickly calls your bet, there's a good chance you're being slow-played. Of course, this all comes down to reading your opponent, but since slow-playing is so common at today's poker tables, most likely if someone is checking to you and representing a weak hand, they probably have a strong hand. The average poker player's strategy doesn't go much deeper than "play weak when you're strong and vice versa." Since you're reading this book, your strategy does go deeper than this, and you'll have no problem figuring out when you're being slow-played.

If you're called or checked to throughout a hand, most likely you are being slow-played. If your opponent waits until fifth street to make a big bet, you're almost definitely being slow-played. Unless you've made what you consider to be a very strong hand, it's probably wise to fold in this situation.

The dangers of slow-playing at work are fewer in number, but just as dangerous as their poker counterparts. Taking an idea to someone else if your boss has passed on it could cause your boss to feel you're going over his head or stepping out of line. Your boss could also get defensive and attempt to steal the project by going to the brass and telling them that he has had the same idea in development for some time and was waiting for the right time to present it. Anytime you present a new idea either to your company or to your industry, some people will react defensively. New ideas can cause people to worry about how that idea might affect their job stability. By slow-playing your idea in a nonthreatening manner, you can prevent others from becoming skittish or defensive.

If you believe that going over your boss's head could damage your position within the company, then you need to figure out how important the project is to you and evaluate it in greater depth. Going ahead with your plan regardless would be considered an all-in situation, which we'll discuss in detail in the last chapter.

Another danger of slow-playing in business is that you could get a reputation for being greedy. Just like in poker, if you slow-play too often and in the wrong situations, you will get caught with your hand in the cookie jar. If you present your idea with only your personal interests in mind or look like you're using your idea to manage up, it can poison the idea for everyone around you and generally hurt your table image. Make sure that every idea, project, or deal that you bring to the table has just as much, if not more, of a benefit for your company as it does for you personally.

While slow-playing is often an obvious tell at the poker table, it's just as obvious in business. Anytime you see someone going out of their way to represent a weak hand, chances are they're downplaying their true strength. Anytime you see someone downplaying the importance of a project or deal, chances are they need the deal a lot more than they are letting on. Even though it's obvious and somewhat amateurish, most people in business and poker will act weak when they are strong, and vice versa. Think of it as the easiest tell to spot, and use this to your advantage whenever possible.

Slow-playing on its own won't make you a great player; it is simply a useful tactic that—if applied in the right circumstance—can be the correct strategy to employ. Relying on slow-playing too often will only hurt you. Most big-time players achieve greatness by learning how to win consistently and in many situations, they don't need pocket aces to help them score the big pots. While pocket aces are nice, they're not a reason to go all in any more than they are a reason to play with deceit or greed.

....

THE SHOWDOWN

**Conceal the true strength of your strongest hands.
Play these hands slowly and patiently—but do it
rarely, and only with the strongest of hands.**

....

TREAT YOUR CAREER AS A TOURNAMENT
The Final Table

Few things are more important in business or poker than being prepared for success. It may sound like a strange concept: being *prepared for success*. After all, why would anyone need to be prepared for something they work every day to achieve? In fact, hasn't your entire career, in many ways, been a long series of preparations for success? Of course. We all strive for success in our careers each and every day. The question here is: are you prepared for what's going to happen when you actually reach that level of success?

Let's take a look at this concept from the poker side of things.

You're playing in a No-Limit Hold 'Em tournament. You've played tightly for the first few hours, won a few big pots, and built up a decent-sized chip stack. You're on the top half of the leader board and feeling good about your position. In fact, so far you've been playing what you consider to be your best poker, your A-game. You've been diligently asking yourself the five questions every half-hour (see rule 3), and you're comfortable with the competition around you, confident that you have what it takes to last deep into the tournament.

There are only a few tables left, and if you play wisely you might find yourself at the final table. Who knows, you could even win the damn thing. For the next hour you catch a long series of amazing hands. The opponents at your table groan in disbelief at your incredible streak of good luck. You're catching trips and flushes like you own the patent on them. But luck isn't going to be enough to get you to the final table. You're going to have to use some strategy as well.

Now the game is down to the final thirty players. Only three tables left. Everyone who makes it to the final two tables lands in the money, meaning they win at least the amount they spent entering into the tournament, but usually more. No one wants to be one of the ten people to last this long in the tournament only to walk away with nothing. Because of this, everyone plays extraordinarily tightly; no one wants to catch a loss that's going to buy them a one-way ticket home. You take stock of the situation and formulate a strategy. If everyone is going to play tightly, afraid of playing any hand that's going to put them to an all-in decision, that means it's going to be very easy for you to steal pots if you play a bit more loosely. Therefore, you decide to play loosely and aggressively. Luckily, you have a pretty big stack, so you're not at too much of a risk of getting put all in by anyone.

Your strategy pays off and your stack grows and grows with

each hand. Players are folding good hands to your bad hands, unwilling to take any risk in a pot unless they have the complete nuts. Before you know it, you have one of the biggest stacks in the tournament, and the floor man is ushering you to the final table, giving you a five-minute break before the competition continues.

The final table.

You've never made it this far in a tournament in your entire life. It's going to be you versus the nine best players in this tournament. In fact, you're going to be playing against nine of the best players in your city.

You sit down at the final table and check out your competition. You've seen almost all of these guys at the casino before. These are the guys who are *always* playing. While you have time to play only once or twice a week, these guys play around the clock. In fact, you've never been to the casino when these guys *weren't* playing. They practically live there. From what you've heard, these are some of the best players around. Even though this isn't a big money tournament, it's one of the biggest tourneys in your area and big enough to draw the best players around.

You've always wondered what the final table would feel like, what it would play like, and now you're about to find out.

Unfortunately, you're in for a rude awakening.

The final table is going to be tough. *Really tough.* These guys are going to be playing at a level you're not used to playing at, and they're going to be able to sustain that level of play longer than you. Your opponents are guys who almost always make it to the final table. They're used to the pressure, the cutthroat tactics, and the mental fatigue. More importantly, they're not intimidated by *you*.

You've always wondered what it would be like to play with the top-level players, but now that you're here, you're not sure if you've got what it takes. You start questioning if you even belong at the final table. Are you prepared for this?

In business, progressing through your career is much like progressing through a poker tournament. As long as you've set a goal for yourself and figured out what it's going to take to feel like a success in your career, you most likely have a metaphorical final table you're striving to get to. All of us are working diligently to reach our final table, but not all of us are ready for the change in game play that will take place once we get there. Will you be ready?

Whether your final table means reaching an executive position in your company, heading your own start-up business, becoming a manager or team leader, or simply getting a promotion, once you reach the next plateau in your career, you're going to find out that you can't play the game the same way that you played it before. It's important that you be prepared for this next step, and there's no time like the present to get ready for it.

You never quite know when you're going to be placed at the final table; it can happen very quickly, especially if you're a top-notch player to begin with. You have to prepare yourself mentally *before* you get to the final table so you'll be focused and confident when it eventually happens.

When you enter a poker tournament, you must always be prepared to make it to the final table. Whatever your business career goal is, you must always be prepared for winning. Once you've reached the final table you'll be playing on a level you've never played on before. The game will change. When thinking of your career as a tournament, you've got to ask yourself: *am I prepared to make it to the final table?*

Back in 1995, when I was working for Electronic Arts (EA), my task was to introduce video game software to the Chinese market. At that point in time, there were no legitimate software companies selling their products to the Chinese market. The entire Chinese video game market was pirated, from the games to the console systems. Not only was every game and game system being pirated and sold illegally, but they were being sold for less than it would actually cost to manufacture these games legally. The pirates had a stranglehold on the market—a near monopoly. Who would pay for a game from a licensed software company when they could get the same game on the street corner for even less than it would cost for a licensed software company to manufacture it? No one dared enter their games legally into the Chinese market—it just wasn't profitable. Yet EA decided to change this; they decided they wanted to see if they could make it profitable, and they sent me in to make it happen.

This was the first time I had ever done something on this scale. Before I started working for EA I had experience in venture capital, experience with my LapSaver business (my start-up company), and experience in investments, but I had never run a group for a large company like this before. I had never been in charge of taking a major brand-name product to market—and in a foreign, untested market to boot! Not only had I never taken on a task of this magnitude before, but most of my team was green as well—all all local Chinese businesspeople who had no experience in selling video games to a Chinese market. How could they? No one but pirates had experience in the Chinese video game market because it had never been done legitimately. It was all new territory, for China, for EA, for my team, and for me.

And just before I was to start, I froze. We spent months researching, learning everything about the Chinese market, getting the logistics down on how we would actually manufacture the software, package it, and distribute it. But after that was figured out, everything else was pure guesswork. We were reaching out in the dark. What was a good price point for the software? What was the best way to market the games? How many units should we manufacture? How many units would we sell? What was the best way to get the games into the hands of the people who want it the most: the gamers?

I believed in what we were doing, I knew it was possible, and I knew that it was up to me to make it happen—but I had no idea what to do. This was the farthest I had ever progressed in the tournament that was my career, this was a final table situation. Was I ready for this? Was I prepared for my final table?

Many of us know where we'd like to end up in our careers, what type of salary we'd like to be making, what type of position we'd like to hold, and what level of responsibility we'd like to take on. But not all of us are ready for actually having all of these things thrust upon us. Some people, when they finally get it, choke under the pressure or discover that it's not quite what they thought it would be, and that they really don't want it after all. Be careful what you wish for!

To prevent "choking" when you finally make it to the big leagues, the key is to train yourself to be aware. In chapter 3 we discussed the five questions you should ask yourself regularly in order to stay sharp and maintain a high level of game play. But when you've made it to the final table, or when you've been promoted to a higher position within your company, you're going to find yourself to be a small fish in a big pond. Your opponents are going to be playing at a higher level than you've ever played at before. Plus, they're going to be used to playing at that level and you're not. Until you get used to this new level of play, your usual five questions aren't going to be enough.

Think of it this way: You can't enter your Honda into a race with Ferraris and expect your usual tune-ups to be sufficient. You're going to have to make some major changes in order to keep up with the competition. Being aware and being prepared for these major changes will give you an edge over the competition and make your transition to the final table that much smoother. In this chapter we'll cover the three major changes within a game that take place when you're suddenly moved to a higher level of competition.

Today, the legal video game market in China is a several hundred million dollar a year market, where major software competitors thrive in a healthy consumer environment. I was able to find a way to take that next step, to look within and find the courage to make a leap of faith into a market that was untested, with a product that was up against some fierce competition by the software pirates. I was able to successfully compete at my final table.

At first we tried to work with the pirates, in the hopes of finding a way to coexist within the same market, but we were simply unable to compete with the low prices the pirates were willing to sell their software for. The pirates were selling their bootlegged PC CD-ROM games for US$1, which was less than what it cost for us to legitimately manufacture our games, let alone make a profit on them. In order to make a dent in the Chinese video game market we would have to create a superior product and, hopefully, find a consumer base willing to spend more on that product. We knew we would have to offer something that the pirates were unable to offer.

For the most part, the PC CD-ROM games that the pirates were selling were bootlegged copies of American games, and because of this they were usually in English for English-speaking gamers. On top of this, the instruction manuals, often integral to the game—especially with the more complicated games—were never included with the pirated games. EA China would offer localized instruction manuals with all of their games, and in many cases, even localized games themselves, all painstakingly translated from the original English into Chinese.

When a game was purchased from the pirates, all the buyer got was the bootlegged PC CD-ROM itself and a small plastic sleeve in which to hold it. Our games would come in large, nicely designed boxes, perfect for displaying on a shelf in the same way one would exhibit a favorite book or a DVD. Offering nicely designed boxes turned our products into collectibles, worthy of displaying and showing off to friends. The pirates didn't offer this.

Finally, we guaranteed that our games would work. When buying a pirated PC CD-ROM game, one would often come home to find a nonworking game, or even a game with a virus hidden in the software that could damage the computer. Our games were guaranteed to work, sanctioned by the Chinese government, and completely safe to install on any computer.

While taking these steps wasn't enough to put a stop to the pirates for good, it proved that there was a viable market for legitimate video game software in China. We sold our products for around US $15, fourteen dollars more than the pirates, yet we were able to move a good deal of units because of our superior product. There were enough Chinese gamers in the market who were interested in translated instruction manuals, collectible boxes, and guaranteed software to make EA China a successful business venture.

You see, there was no single element that made our product launch a success, no single answer to any of the myriad questions we had that helped us put all of the pieces together, but being aware of the changes that took place at this new level of my career, at this new level of responsibility, made a huge difference in my team's ability to succeed. The seed for the process of training myself to be aware, the process laid out in this chapter, was planted in my head during my experiences with EA China.

Once you've made it to the final table, you'll be playing on a much broader playing field. You are no longer simply a doer at your job, you are now a decision maker. You're going to be surrounded by people who were, or who still are, your seniors within the company. These are people who have a lot more experience playing at this high level than you have. If you're going to survive, you're going to have to be hyperaware of everything that is going on around you. The major changes you'll need to be aware of include the elevated importance of blinds, chip stack, and position in every decision you make.

What do blinds, chip stack, and position have to do with the final table of your career? The same as they do with the final table of a poker tournament.

THE IMPORTANCE OF BLINDS

In both business and No-Limit Hold 'Em, there is no such thing as a free ride. There is always something at stake, there is always some risk involved in simply just sitting down at a poker table or waking up and going in to work. While you don't have to play every hand that you're dealt at the poker table, you do have to pay an ante twice per round. These antes are known as the small blind and the big blind, and they travel together, always to the immediate left of the button, side by side like a pair of hungry wolves looking to devour your chips. The higher the stakes at the table, or the further you've advanced in a tournament, the higher the blinds and the more chips you're going to forfeit whether you're playing the hands or not.

The higher you advance in your career, the higher the blinds become as well, meaning the higher the stakes become. If you're at a low level in your company, there is less expected of you and less responsibility on your shoulders, and fewer people are keeping an eye out for every mistake you make, but at the same time there is less to win because with small blinds come small pots. Getting to the top of your company or being a manager of a team is like sitting at the final table of a tournament with the blinds reaching $10,000 or $20,000 a round—you can't sit idly by and wait for the obvious hands to play; you have to make big choices, take big risks, and play lots of hands. If you wait too long, you're going to get blinded to death and run out of chips. While waiting for the perfect hand, you'll lose all of your chips round by round as the blinds slowly suck you dry.

When the blinds get high, not only do you have to take action more often than you do at lower blinds, but your actions have to be done with more confidence and with greater aggression. You're no longer playing in a $10 house game or in the rebuy phase of a $50 tournament, you're in the big leagues now. You have to think of the final table as your own private World Series of Poker. Heck, maybe you even won a satellite tournament, got a ticket into the World Series of Poker, and now find yourself sitting at the final table. It's happened to amateurs before. It happened to Chris Moneymaker and he was even able to win the thing. Why? Because *he was prepared to make it to the final table.* He got a little bit lucky, but mostly he was able to ramp up his level of play to match the greatest players in the world, even though he had never played at that level in his life. How? He was mentally prepared for success.

That's what it takes.

When the blinds go up you're going to have to take bigger risks. You're going to have to play more hands. You're going to have to make more decisions, and you're going to have to fight for each win. There's a reason the people at the top positions in most companies rarely last longer than a few years. Most high-level executives move around within their industries like they're playing a game of musical chairs. Gone are the days when CEOs lived and died with their companies. Why is this? Because in today's global marketplace the competition is higher than it's ever been. The blinds are so high that many executives live or die by each and every decision they make. Whether they are asked to leave, take it upon themselves to resign, or get snatched up by a company with a better offer, today's high-level executives play a lot of hands, and because of the level of the blinds, each hand carries a lot of weight.

THE IMPORTANCE OF CHIP STACKS

In almost every situation in my life I'm evaluating chip stacks. It's something that has become second nature to me, but I also enjoy doing it. Calculating chip stacks is part of the fun of looking at my career as a game of poker. I also find it to be a very beneficial way of approaching challenging meetings, phone calls, interviews, and almost every facet of my business life. The times in my life when

I've been bumped up to a higher level in my job or found myself sitting in a boardroom with a group of high-level executives, I always take the time to formulate the chip stacks in the room. Who is the big stack? Who is the small stack? How are the chip stacks going to affect the meeting?

But how exactly does the chip stack translate into the business world? It doesn't necessarily have anything to do with who makes the higher salaries. It has more to do with who has the most leverage, who has the most influence and power, whose personality gets the most positive attention, who garners the highest expectation, and whose opinion the boss or the CEO respects the most. Chip stacks can take on many forms, yet at the same time, it's also very intuitive and easy to determine.

The concept of chip stacks can be applied anywhere and in any situation. There are even chip stacks to be found in front of your family when you sit down to dinner. Maybe no one takes the last piece of steak because Dad always gets it. Maybe no one interrupts Mom when she's talking. Maybe Junior is able to boss his sister around and no one ever calls him on it or punishes him. These are the equivalents of chip stacks at a poker table.

You may not actually see the chips in front of your family members, but when Dad makes the kids do the dishes, he has pushed his big stack onto the table and they have folded their cards, knowing for sure they have no chance at winning this hand. Imagine if the kids told Dad to do the dishes. They would have metaphorically pushed their chip stacks onto the table, causing Dad to laugh as he slides his big, towering chip stack toward the middle. The kids would have no choice but to fold—their stacks are simply too small to risk on such a weak hand.

Power, respect, expectation—these are the core manifestations of chip stacks. A large chip stack has the power to push opponents around. A large chip stack forces opponents to respect your decisions and weigh the consequences of moving against you. A large chip stack causes opponents to expect authority and strong action from you.

On the flip side, a small chip stack has none of these things going for it. Every move a small stack makes puts it in jeopardy of being put all in by the larger stacks. For a small stack to make a move in a world of large stacks, it must be extremely confident that it will succeed, knowing that if it fails it will be completely out of chips.

When you are moved to your final table, whatever that final table may be, you are always going to be forced to prove your merit. In order to be accepted by the more experienced players, your first few moves had better be strong ones that achieve positive results or else you're going to be put all in and risk the possibility of losing all your chips. On the other hand, the small stack can't last forever when the blinds are high, so you're going to have to play a hand eventually. You just better hope it's a strong one.

If you fail to take chip stacks into consideration in every business situation, you are putting yourself at risk of making an uneducated decision. At the final table of a poker tournament, you wouldn't play your hand the same against a small stack as you would against a big stack, so there's no excuse for doing it at the final table of your career either.

THE IMPORTANCE OF POSITION

Few things at the poker table are more important than position. The closer you are to the button, the more information you will have when it is time to make a decision. Having the opportunity to observe your opponents' actions before you decide how to play your hand allows you to play a wider variety of hands, to make bets leveraged by your position, and to better conceal the strength of your hand. Generally, it is true that the closer you are to the button, the higher your chances of winning the pot.

At the final table in most tournaments you will find that the majority of pots are entered by only two or three players. It is rare that you find a large multiway pot when the blinds are high and the stakes are large, such as they are toward the end of a tournament. More often than not, it is the blinds and/or the button who are the ones fighting over a given pot. Because of the button's advantageous position, the player sitting at the button has the ability to take larger risks in the hands he or she plays. Because the button is the last to act, it's that much harder for the other players to get a read on the button position's hand; therefore, control of the game will usually be left up to the button.

Players will often check to the button and wait to see what the button does. Every bet placed by a player outside of the button is done with a tinge of fear. After all, you never know when the button might swoop in and make a large enough reraise to scare you out of the pot. In poker, the button controls the flow of the game and all decisions go through him or her before the game is allowed to progress.

Things are no different in the world of business.

I've always found it interesting that at any given meeting the head of the table is usually reserved for the person who has the biggest chip stack or the person who is planning on leading the meeting—as if sitting in a certain position at a table somehow gives a person more power or commands greater respect. As arbitrary as it may seem from an outsider's perspective, the fact remains that in meetings and in business deals, the person sitting at the head of the table commands the most power. The person sitting at the head of the table is the button. All questions are deferred to the button. The general flow of the meeting is led by the button. Even the moment when the meeting is to end is decided by the person sitting at the button. The button is power.

Because the head of the table is generally considered the position of power, it's essential you understand its importance and learn how to use it to your advantage. Not understanding the importance of position in the higher levels of your career is as dangerous as not understanding the position of the button at the final table of a poker tournament.

I once worked with a man who, as long as there wasn't a senior member of the team in the room, would always make sure he sat at the head of the table. Whether the meeting was his to lead, whether it was a formal or informal meeting, or whether he was in any way involved in the orchestrating of the meeting, he would always go out of his way to take the position of power. What made it worse was that this guy was pretty junior in the grand scheme of the company. We were all equals in our group, yet he felt the need to separate himself at every opportunity by sitting on the button. Once he was in this seat, his demeanor would completely change. He would become bossy, gain more confidence, and micromanage, even though it didn't make sense for him to be doing so. His actions were really bothersome to the rest of his team who expected—and rightfully so—a more democratic process.

Even though his bully-style actions didn't immediately affect his standing in the company (since he wasn't so dumb as to attempt this stunt when one of the senior executives was in the room), it became obvious to me just how important and influential position really is in the world of business.

Some colleagues, such as the man I just spoke of, are naturally drawn to the head of the table. This is the poker equivalent of acting as if you are the button when sitting away from the button. By betting big when you're out of position, you tell the rest of the table that you either have a great hand or that you're trying to steal the pot. If you don't actually have a great hand to back up your bet (which my ex-colleague certainly didn't), you're going to get a reputation for trying to steal pots and acting like a bully. Do this too many times and you'll find that most people are hesitant to enter pots with you, giving you very few opportunities to take down any significant-sized pots.

If I have my whole team, of which I'm the leader, coming in for a meeting, I will usually sit at the head of the table, mostly because it's expected. But if I'm at a meeting where the leader of the meeting isn't obvious, I'll choose to sit elsewhere so as not to give others the impression that I *need* to sit at the head of the table. I don't want to be seen as a bully within my company—it's not the table image I want to create in my working environment. There's a time and a place for being the bully, and for me, that time is rarely with my colleagues.

Also, you don't necessarily have to be sitting at the head of the table to lead the meeting. In poker this would be called *buying the button*. A player to the right of the button makes a bet he believes to be large enough to get the button to fold. If all the players between him and the button, including the button, fold their cards, then that player has effectively bought the button. Now this person is the last to act at the end of every betting round and has taken unto himself the same power once bestowed on the button.

If you believe that you, and only you, can effectively lead a meeting, or if you feel that the meeting is being steered off track, then you need to buy the button by interjecting yourself into the conversation and taking the reins. You'll find that most great leaders don't need to sit at the head of the table to garner respect. In fact, I've found that most of the great business leaders I've come in contact with often let a more junior member of their team take the head seat, in the hopes of inspiring greater confidence and a stronger leadership role in that person. Letting other team members control the flow of a meeting can be a very effective managing tool, as long as you know how to buy the button when necessary.

Blinds, chip stacks, and position have the ability to significantly affect the way you see your colleagues and competitors—and how they see you. Whether you are sitting down to the final table of a poker tournament or being promoted to a new level in your career, being aware of the importance of blinds, chip stacks, and position becomes an essential survival skill.

Looking back on my experiences with EA China, even though it took place a few years before I was introduced to the game of No-Limit Hold 'Em, I now see how I utilized these concepts without even being aware that I was doing so. Because it was my first time leading a team of such a large size with a project of such great magnitude, it was imperative that I act quickly and decisively. The blinds were so high that if I waited too long before introducing our product line to the Chinese market, EA would lose faith in me as a leader and our team would fall apart. I knew I had to act quickly.

My chip stack, on the other hand, was small. The software pirates had all of the power. They were the ones with a firm grip on the video game consumer. They had prices we couldn't match. I knew that if our product line was going to succeed, we would have to offer something the pirates didn't. We would have to offer a better product. The only way to build our chip stack was to make a move against the pirates by representing a stronger hand.

Finally, I felt as though my position was strong. EA, the world's largest software developer, was behind me. I had their support and their brand name to help give our product line the best chance possible in this new, untested market. Because of EA's respected brand name, I knew that we were in a great position to take the leadership role in the video game consumer market. After all, who is the consumer going to trust more for a quality product: the largest software developer on the planet or a guy selling bootleg video games on the corner? When it came to position, I knew we had the upper hand.

Being aware of these three factors helped me to mentally prepare for my final table. I knew my team had to act quickly, I knew we had to offer a superior product, and I knew that having EA behind us put us in a strong position to succeed. All three of these factors combined to help our team to attain its goal and to make a considerable dent in the Chinese legitimate video game market.

While being aware of these three concepts before you reach your final table can never hurt you, it becomes utterly necessary when you find yourself the small fish in the big pond. After all, to make a name for yourself in this new world you're going to have to take risks, but your risks can't be thoughtless or impulsive, they have to be risks calculated on your most educated guesses. Only by taking note of the blinds, the chip stacks, and position in every situation you come across or every colleague you interact with, will you put yourself in a position to succeed and progress.

Another great, exciting element of moving to the final table is that you're playing with the best players you've ever played with. This is when you're really going to learn and grow as a player. This is when you're going to be stretched to your full potential, so eventually it won't feel like a stretch at all. Play enough final tables in your life and you'll feel as comfortable playing with the best of them as you would playing with a group of your closest friends.

At the same time, never lose sight of the fact that it's a game. I'm talking about both business *and* poker here. I've always noticed how the tension level can rise exponentially once you reach your final table. Because of this, it's hard to remember, at these higher levels of play, to have fun. While I enjoying taking both poker and business seriously, doing everything I can to play my best and to succeed, it's only because I have fun playing in this fashion that I find it beneficial to me. If you're not able to have fun playing at your final table, then there's no way you're going to bring your A-game.

Also, the fact that you're playing at your final table doesn't mean you should be tiptoeing around your new opponents, afraid to rock the boat because you're the new kid on campus. If you played hard and aggressively in order to get to your final table, you had better play hard and aggressively once you get there. After all, it's what your new competitors will be expecting of you.

If this is your first time at a final table, as long as you've done your best to prepare and you're doing your best to be as aware as you can be, don't be upset if you lose a few hands. Don't even be upset if you lose the whole thing. No one expects you to win the final table your first time around. Take the pressure off of yourself and realize you're sitting at the final table with the best players around. Take a moment to remind yourself that *you deserve to be sitting there*. You are the one who got yourself there, you are the one who did all the work. Perception is reality: *you are ready for the final table*.

And if that doesn't work, think of it this way: if you made it to the final table of the World Series of Poker and found yourself sitting next to Doyle Brunson, even if you lost ... hell, you lost to *Doyle Brunson*.

THE SHOWDOWN

Always be prepared to win. The closer you get to your final table, the more important blinds, chip stacks, and position become.

KNOW WHEN AND HOW TO BLUFF
The Art of Bluffing and Semibluffing

In business and in poker, there are times when it pays to conceal the truth. There are times when the right move is to pretend your hand is stronger than it actually is. At the poker table, there are times when the only way to win is to lie straight to someone's face. In the boardroom, there are times when the only way to win is to exhibit full confidence, no matter what you're pitching or selling. This is what is commonly referred to as *bluffing*.

Sometimes you bluff because you have no other options, or *outs*, as they're called in the poker world. At other times, you bluff because you have the strength and the position to do so. There are even times when you bluff simply because you know you can get away with it. Knowing when and how to bluff are two of the most important lessons a player can learn in business and in poker. A properly executed bluff is a necessary tool in any great player's repertoire.

In this chapter I'm going to look at bluffing from every angle. I'm going to cover why you bluff, how you bluff, and when you bluff. You'll learn the difference between bluffing and semibluffing, or as they translate to the business world: lying and stretching. On top of that I'll discuss the importance of integrity and solid business ethics.

In the business world, a good bluffer can bluff his way into his dream job. In the poker world, a good bluffer can take down a big pot whether he's got a few outs or is drawing completely dead.

Get ready to learn the true art of the bluff.

WHAT IS BLUFFING?

In poker, bluffing is a way of persuading your opponents into folding their hands by representing a strong hand when you actually have a weak one. It's holding a 2-4 in your hand, yet betting like you've got pocket aces. There are two different kinds of bluffs: a bluff and a semibluff.

A bluff means you're playing with nothing. You've got almost no chance of winning the pot if the hand were to come down to the showdown, yet you still believe you can win the pot by convincing your opponent that his or her hand is weaker than yours. This convincing usually takes the form of a large bet.

Because you're forgoing your cards and relying purely on the power of your influence, bluffing is by far the riskiest move in all of poker. All you have going for you is your chip stack, your position, your table image, and your courage. Because your cards are so weak, you've got no way of backing up your bet if you were to get called. Bluffing is one of the few instances where you're not looking for a call—you're betting purely out of the hope that your opponent will fold his or her hand. In fact, when you bluff you might as well not even have any cards at all. When you bluff you play the player sitting across from you, not the cards in your hand. Bluffing is a purely psychological play.

There is a true art to bluffing. Some people are great at it, it's as if they were born to do it. That is not to say that these people are born liars exactly, but when it comes to game strategy, these people have a natural poker face and an innate ability to deceive. Natural-born bluffers give up no information with their body language or their betting patterns. As long as these types know the appropriate time to bluff and the appropriate way to bluff, they'll find that the chips come readily and the game is theirs to lose.

Some of us, on the other hand, have a hard time bluffing. It doesn't come naturally to us at all. Our hands shake when we reach for our chips, we lean forward when we place our bets, or we bet too big, showing the weakness of our hand by overbetting the pot. Some of us even feel a tinge of guilt when we bluff, having been properly taught in our youths never to deceive our fellow man. Some of us view bluffing as a form of lying.

Well, guess what? Bluffing *is* lying, and when it comes to No-Limit Hold 'Em, lying is not only accepted—it's encouraged. No one is going to fault you for bluffing them out of their pocket queens when you were representing kings. They may hate you, but they won't fault you. In fact, they'll probably even respect your play, and run it over and over in their minds for hours on end, trying to figure out how exactly you pulled it off so at their next game they can attempt the same move on some other chump. In poker, the great bluffers are also highly respected and highly successful players.

In business, though, it's a whole different story.

There is so much bluffing going on in business it's almost unbelievable. In fact, I'd go so far as to say that there may be no stronger parallel to be found between the world of poker and business than there is in bluffing. Let me give you a few examples of the bluffing found every day in the business world, starting all the way at the bottom of the food chain and working way up to the top.

BLUFFING IN THE BUSINESS WORLD

Some people bluff when they apply for a job, fudging their histories on their résumés in order to deceive a potential boss into hiring them on false pretenses. But what happens when that boss checks up on your references and learns you're not the person he or she believed you to be?

Some people bluff in business when they make promises they can't keep in order to persuade clients to sign deals or entice colleagues to partner up with them. But what happens when all the promises they've made turn out to be lies and that trust is forever broken?

Some people bluff in business when they try to scare off their opponents by making threats they can't back up. But what happens when those threats turn out to be false and their rivals reveal their scare tactics to the public?

Some companies bluff when they claim to have products or technologies ready that they haven't fully developed yet. But what happens when their customers find out the truth behind their lies? How do they get their customers back once they've switched over to a more honest company's line of products?

Some CEOs bluff when they tell the press they have no knowledge of insider trading or tax fraud taking place within their company walls. But what happens when they're brought in front of the judge and made to swear under oath regarding the truth behind their company's finances?

These are just a few of the examples of the bluffing that takes place in the business world each and every day. In this fast-paced, highly competitive, overcrowded global marketplace in which we live today, the temptation to lie and to bluff can be overwhelming. While making a full bluff in poker may be a smart way to play the game, in business a full bluff is *never* the right move. The great companies and the great players in business don't need to bluff in order to profit or succeed.

In business, the people who make a full bluff—a bluff that is an outright lie with no chance of being backed up in any way—almost always lose in the end. When you bluff in poker, the worst-case scenario is that you lose all your chips. When you bluff in business, the worst case scenario is that you gain a reputation for being a dishonest person, lose the trust of your industry, possibly lose your job, or even risk going to prison.

Today, a full bluff in the business world gets more news coverage, and is taken more seriously, than ever before—and rightfully so. Corporate fraud, a recent epidemic in the business world, can have serious ramifications for the executives involved. Corporate executives such as Andrew Fastow of Enron, Timothy and John Rigas of Adelphia, and Bernard Ebbers of WorldCom all received jail time in the past few years for charges of corporate fraud.

These types of white-collar crimes used to be punished with the judicial equivalent of a slap on the wrists, but with executives like Bernard Ebbers getting sentenced to twenty-five years in prison, full bluffs in the business world are no longer a laughing matter. While cases like these are the most extreme examples of business bluffs (obviously not all business bluffs lead to jail time), it's important to realize that whether you're the CEO of a *Fortune 500* company or you're just out of college and applying for an entry-level position, the potential rewards of pulling off a full bluff never equal the severe ramifications of getting caught in one.

The only type of bluff I recommend in the business world is the semibluff. In fact, I don't just recommend the semibluff; I believe that if you don't understand the importance of the semibluff, you'll never make it as a player in today's economy.

Just as there is a true art to bluffing at the poker table, there is a true art to semibluffing in the business world. Before we get into how to semibluff, let me explain exactly what it is.

WHAT IS SEMIBLUFFING?

When semibluffing, you have a hand you are almost positive isn't the strongest hand at the table, yet you believe that by making a strong enough bet you will be able to scare out the rest of the competition and win the pot. Unlike a normal bluff, when you semibluff, you're not playing with a truly worthless hand—you have at least some kind of a hand. Whether you have bottom or middle pair, a straight or flush draw, or maybe you've even made a straight or a flush (yet have reason to believe your hand is not the strongest at the table), you're not playing with a completely weak hand. When you semibluff, there's even a chance that your hand could eventually become the strongest hand if you were to get the right cards on the turn or on the river.

When you semibluff in poker, you're not drawing completely dead—there's still a chance you could win the pot, but the odds aren't with you. Therefore, you've got to make some sort of a bluff if you want to secure the pot. You're not quite bluffing all out, you're just sort of *exaggerating* the value of your hand.

The main difference between bluffing and semibluffing in poker is that if your semibluff were to get called by your opponent, there would still be a chance you could actually win the pot based on the strength of your hand. When you semibluff, the odds are stacked slightly more in your favor then when you bluff straight out. A semibluff is a much safer bluff.

One of the main keys to succeeding in business is to always remain ethical. If you're caught in a lie, your integrity will forever be in question. Without integrity, you'll have a hard time getting people to work with you or for you. Full bluffs in business rarely work, and when they do, the risk involved in making them rarely outweighs the consequences of getting caught. In poker-speak this is called *having the worst of it*, which is the same as being on the low side of a win–lose ratio—not the place any self-respecting player wants to find himself, either in business or in poker.

To act as though you have skills you've never put to the test, or to imply that your skills are stronger than they actually are, is different than a full bluff. If you were to take on a project larger than you'd ever taken on before and your boss were to ask you if you thought you could handle it, answering yes wouldn't exactly be a bluff—it would be a semibluff. If your boss were then to ask you if you'd ever led a project like this before and you were to say yes, then that would be a full bluff and could land you in some serious hot water if your boss were to find out the truth. If you've got *some of the skills* needed for a certain task and trust that you'll be able to stretch your abilities in order to get the job done, then semibluffing is the correct play. In fact, semibluffing is one of the most common and most effective ways in which people propel themselves to the next level of their careers.

In business the difference between a bluff and a semibluff is very clear. As long as you honestly have the confidence in yourself to achieve what you set out to achieve, it is acceptable to semibluff. Implying that your hand is stronger than it is in order to be given the opportunity to prove yourself is more a reflection on your courage and self-confidence than it is on your ability to manipulate or lie. If you have absolutely no idea how you're going to pull off what you've promised to do or have to blatantly lie or deceive in order to get what you want, then that's a straight-up bluff and an unethical move in the business world.

Semibluffing in business is about recognizing your talent, envisioning yourself in a better position in your career, and presenting yourself in such a way that the higher-ups feel comfortable giving you that greater responsibility.

Now that we've explained the vital differences between bluffing and semibluffing, let's get into the *how* and the *when* of both of them.

WHEN TO BLUFF

Before you learn how to bluff, you have to learn *when* to bluff. So when exactly should you bluff at the poker table? The simple answer: whenever you can. Knowing when these opportune moments have arrived is the tricky part. Luckily, there are four simple factors you can use to gauge your ability to effectively bluff: chip stack, position, table image, and your read on your opponents.

Chip Stack

The rule of thumb in poker is that the bigger your chip stack, the easier it is to bluff. If you've got a massive pile of chips in front of you, then you can put any player at the table to a serious decision whenever that player is in a hand with you. If you have a large chip stack, you'll have a much easier time bluffing. The simple fact that a player would rather fold than jeopardize a large percentage of his or her chips on the chance that you actually have a strong hand is often reason enough to bluff. Be careful, though—bluff too many times and you're going to get caught with your hand in the cookie jar. But hey, what do you care? You've got a giant stack of chips! Bluffing with the big stack is very similar to playing like the Bully (see rule 2, p. 29). It's all about pushing the table around and stealing chips whenever you feel that a player has shown weakness.

So how do you know when your opponents are showing weakness? Your opponents can reveal weaknesses in a few different ways. Checking is usually either a sign of weakness or a sign your opponent might be setting a trap, obvious though it may be. If your opponent simply calls your bet as opposed to raising, that can also be interpreted as a sign of weakness. When you sense weakness, you can bluff by making a bet large enough to scare out the competition. Whenever you're the big stack, you should do your best to take advantage of these situations and bluff whenever possible to increase your profits. But be careful—do it too many times and you'll have a hard time getting anyone to play against you in later hands. And remember, behaving like this at the poker table is acceptable, but this type of aggressive, cutthroat playing in the business world can lead to a bad reputation and a lack of integrity.

The smaller your stack, then the smaller your chance of pulling off an effective bluff. If you have only a few chips left, or if you're the small stack at your table, most players with a decent hand will call any raise you make, since it won't be costing them much to keep you honest and make sure you're not bluffing.

In most poker games you'll find one player with a small stack who is waiting for his Alamo hand, meaning the first semidecent hand that comes along that he can go all in on in the hopes of doubling up his small stack. Most players will assume that anyone with a small stack who raises or goes all in is doing so with an Alamo hand and will usually call the small stack's bet as long as their hand is average or above. This is why there's almost no way to bluff with a small stack.

Position

Position also plays a large role in your ability to effectively pull off a bluff. The stronger your position—meaning the closer you are to the button—the more information you'll have when it's your time to make a decision. If all the players before you have checked or showed weakness, a good-sized bet might be enough to win the pot right then and there, regardless of the cards in your hand.

To bet strongly from a late position when the rest of the field has either checked or made a small bet is considered a position raise, meaning you raised only because you were in the position to do so. Be careful—a lot of players are aware of the position raise and may call you or reraise you purely because they assume you raised only because of your strong position. Reading your opponents correctly in this situation is vital. If you've got a large stack and the courage to make a big reraise, you may be able to force your opponent to reconsider his opinion of your position raise and to fold his hand before he has to go all in against you.

Table Image

Your table image is also a very important factor in deciding when you can pull off an effective bluff. If you've been playing tightly all night long—meaning you've only been playing hands in the good to great category—then it shouldn't be too hard to slip a few bad hands in there and pretend they are strong in order to win a few pots. If you get caught doing this, your whole table image for that night will be ruined, but most likely if you do it only a few times throughout the night, it should be pretty easy for you to successfully bluff a few big pots.

When it comes to table image, the bottom line is that the more you get caught bluffing, the harder it is going to be to bluff again. If you plan on doing a bit of bluffing—which you almost always should—make sure you create a table image for yourself that does not cause your opponents to constantly second guess the strength of your hand. You want your bets to be respected at the table, so if your opponents think half of your bets are bluffs, the power of your bets will be significantly diminished and your chance of bluffing will be reduced to nil.

Your Read on Your Opponents

Aside from your chip stack, position, and table image, the final factor in knowing when to bluff is having a solid read on your opponents. By watching how the other players at your table play, you'll get all the information you need to decide who is safe to bluff against and who is not. The *calling station*—the player who calls almost every bet regardless of the cards in his hand—shouldn't be bluffed against. The Wild Man, with his loose cannon raising and his emotional game play, should never be bluffed against either.

On the flip side, Mr. Tight/Aggressive is great to bluff against.

As long as he hasn't caught a great hand, which he'll make very apparent by making a large bet, Mr. Tight/Aggressive will almost always fold to your bluff with anything outside of a great hand. This is a wonderful way to pick up a bunch of small to medium-sized pots.

Anytime you pick up on a weakness in your opponent's play or feel that you have a solid read on when he's likely to fold his hand, it is the correct time to make a bluff and steal the pot.

Knowing when to bluff is the only tricky part to bluffing. If you bluff at the wrong time and get caught, you risk losing a chunk of your chips and will have a hard time bluffing again for a good while. While the consequences are nowhere near as steep as they are in the business world, knowing when to bluff can give you an edge over the competition and help significantly increase your profits.

Knowing when to make a full bluff in business is easy: NEVER! I'll keep it simple so I don't repeat myself too much: I don't believe in outright bluffing in business. I think it lacks integrity and, in the long run, can only hurt your business and your career. Bottom line: don't bluff in business.

HOW TO BLUFF

This is the easy part. There are many ways to bluff at a poker table. You can bluff by screaming out "Yes!" every time you're dealt a bad hand, although that usually works only against children. Or you can make a well-executed bet. That's all there is to it. While there's no exact science to gauging the perfect size of the bet that is going to scare out your competition, a solid read on your opponents will help you know how many chips to reach back for when you place that bluff bet.

When you bluff, you want your opponents to fold. You're not looking for a call and you're not looking for a raise. You just want them to fold, get out of the hand, give you their chips, and forget the hand ever happened. Because of this, you want to make a large enough bet so that your opponents will call only if they either have a very strong hand or are convinced you are bluffing. Knowing if your opponent has a truly strong hand goes back to your read on your opponents. Only by watching your opponent and learning how he or she plays will you have the know-how to correctly read the strength of his or her hand. Remember, you only want to bluff against a player you believe has either a weak hand or a decent hand, but never against a player you believe has a strong hand.

The size of your bet has a lot do to with disguising your bluff. An extremely large bet can often be read as a desperate attempt to steal the pot, whereas a small bet can often be a very effective bluff since it tricks your opponent into thinking you're trying to "trap" him or her with a strong hand. Once again, knowing how large to make your bet comes down to your read on your opponent. I've always found that a large bet, not a *huge* bet, but maybe 40 to 50 percent of my opponent's chip stack, is usually enough to put the fear of God into anyone holding anything less than a strong hand. As long as you don't have a reputation for bluffing—and you aren't up against an opponent with a great hand—you should be able to pull off a full bluff a handful of times per session and add a solid chunk of change to your bankroll without anyone being the wiser.

Once you pull off that bluff, it is up to you whether or not you want to reveal to your opponents that you bluffed. While flipping your cards over and showing that you just took the pot down with a garbage hand can be fun way to make your opponents feel really stupid, it's generally not the smartest thing to do. Keeping your opponents constantly guessing as to the strength of your hand is a much better strategy than making your opponents resent you and plan your demise. However, there is a time and a place to reveal your bluff. If your bets are getting too much respect, meaning that everyone at the table assumes you play only very strong hands and therefore they fold every time you make a bet, it might be smart to take down a pot with a bluff and show the table your hand so that they know sometimes you do indeed play weaker hands.

How do you bluff in business? Once again: *you don't*. But you do semibluff in business—a lot. So let's get right into that.

HOW TO SEMIBLUFF

When you first start out along your career path you're filled with an optimistic can-do attitude. You want to take on more responsibility, more leadership, a higher salary, a better position, and pretty much anything else you can get your hands on. Every task you take on, you do with a confident "Yes, I can" to your boss. In essence, you semibluff constantly. Even though you may have no idea what you're doing, you know that to turn down any opportunity or responsibility you're handed at such an early stage in your career would reflect badly on you in the eyes of others.

Just like at the beginning of a poker tournament, at the start of your career you steal lots of little blinds, take down a bunch of small pots, and semibluff like crazy to help increase your stack size for the later stages of the tournament. In business, you have to believe in yourself and believe you can accomplish any task you take on, even if you've never done that specific task before. If your boss were to probe a little deeper and ask how much experience you actually had with that specific task, then you would have no choice but to tell the truth. But if your boss simply were to ask you if you feel you're up to the task, you better damn well answer yes.

I can boil my success in business down to a few very important meetings. When it's my time to go in front of the board, or in for a job interview, I know that I have to pitch my idea, or tell the story of my career, by turning it into an *exciting story*. I know that I have to make my product and my career bigger than life. The meetings in which I have been able to capture the imaginations of the executives I was pitching or the potential boss I was interviewing for, have been the most important moments of my business career. Those one-hour meetings can lead to a few years of a great job and/or a few years of new responsibilities and experiences.

It's all about how I present my product or myself. I know that if I simply walk into important meetings and lay out the facts, or explain my point with a straightforward, by-the-numbers presentation, the people I'm pitching to won't feel the incentive to say yes. But if I walk into that meeting full of fire and energy and explain how my product can revolutionize the way they do business or how my management style can completely reinvigorate their company if they were to hire me, then I stand a good chance of getting the green light. I get their imaginations working; I get them excited about the future, about our partnership, and about the potential of whatever it is I'm trying to convince them. Am I lying at all when I do this? Of course not. Am I exaggerating to make my point? A bit. Do I believe I can back up everything I'm saying with results? Definitely. Am I confident that they won't be disappointed in the development of my product or in the quality of my work? One hundred percent.

When I go into these meetings, I don't quite have the hand I'm representing. I don't quite have the two kings I want them to think I have, but I have a middle pair with a bunch of outs, and I believe that in the end my hand will become the strongest, regardless of its actual strength at that particular moment in time.

You see, in poker when you effectively semibluff someone, he lays down his hand believing that you really had him beat. Usually, you don't flip over your cards and show him how stupid his fold was; you smile and say "Good fold" and continue letting him believe he made the right play. All that matters is that your opponent believes he did the right thing and you took down the pot fair and square. The business equivalent of this is that when you semibluff, as long as the person you're semibluffing feels satisfied with his or her decision to say yes to you, it doesn't matter if you had the strongest hand to begin with at all. As long as in the end you can deliver what you promised to deliver, you never need to flip over your cards and show them how weak your hand actually was. You just smile and thank them for putting their faith in you.

Whenever you're up for a promotion or a project, pitching a new product or a new client, you almost always have to do a bit of semibluffing. You want people to feel confident in your abilities or in the potential of your product. If you have a strong background or a strong track record, people will be more inclined to believe your semibluffs. This is the equivalent of having a big stack in poker. If the person you're trying to semibluff knows from past experience that you are a man or woman of your word and that you can be trusted to get the job done, then that person will feel a lot more confident in the strength of your hand and will have no problem folding and giving you the pot, confident that they made the right decision. I never quite represent the nuts (the best possible hand), but I represent a hand definitely worth respecting and worth betting on.

It's important that you don't take semibluffing too far and start guaranteeing things you can never deliver, because that's when a semibluff turns into a straight-up bluff. You never want to take the semibluff to a level you don't feel confident you can back up. With a semibluff, all you're trying to do is assure your opponent how confident you are in yourself. You want to leave the meeting or the interview having convinced them that you have the best plan and are the only person who can get it done.

In poker, the semibluff is done in almost the same way as the regular bluff. The bigger your stack, the stronger your position, the tighter your table image, and the better the read you have on your opponents, then the more effective your semibluff will be. The difference is that with a semibluff you actually have a chance at winning the pot fair and square. Therefore, you can be a bit more lenient in your stack size, position strength, table image, and read on your opponent, since if you do actually get called you still have a chance of pulling out the win. Yet, usually you don't want to get called if you're semibluffing, so my best advice is to treat it like a regular bluff and do your best to make the right-sized bet that's going to force your opponents to fold.

WHY YOU SHOULD SEMIBLUFF IN BUSINESS

By only listing the facts of a given product or idea, you fail to give the person you're pitching to a full vision of the future. By only listing the achievements you've accomplished thus far in your life, you fail to give a possible employer a complete understanding of your potential. In order to fully convince someone of a business venture, you need to give them more than just the "right here, right now" of what you're selling. You need to look into the future for them. You need to get them excited about working with you.

Being able to inspire any person you're talking to is one of the most important aspects of being a successful businessperson. A well-executed semibluff has the ability to paint a vivid picture of the future, whether it be the future of a product, of a deal, or of you yourself. The semibluff is the deal closer.

A solid presentation does a good deal of stretching. It stretches for possibilities just out of its grasp and it convinces that eventually, with a little work, it will be able to grab hold of those possibilities with ease. That stretch, or semibluff, is the final piece that will connect all the pieces of your pitch together and make your presentation a slam dunk.

For some, the ability to semibluff comes naturally, while others have to work at it a bit. One of the great advantages of applying your poker skills to your business life is that it makes concepts like stretching a lot easier to understand for people to whom the concept doesn't come naturally.

Think of it this way: the person you're pitching to believes he has a good hand, but he knows he doesn't have the best possible hand. If you're in the room pitching a product or going in for a job interview, the company you're pitching to obviously believes there are areas they aren't fully taking advantage of and hopes that your product, or you, can help them improve. No company has the full nuts; every company is looking to improve their hand a bit. This is where semibluffing comes in. You have to convince the person you're pitching to that your hand is strong enough for them to bet on. You've got to represent that you have a plan that is going to take the company to greater success. If you're not confident in your plan, then the semibluff quickly becomes an unethical bluff, but if you *are* confident in your plan, then you're going to have to sell your pitch with passion in order to convince them. If stretching doesn't come naturally to you, simply think of it in poker terms: you've got to represent a stronger hand than your opponent if you want to win the pot. That's all it takes.

WHEN TO SEMIBLUFF

When is the right time to semibluff in business? Whenever you honestly believe you can accomplish a task yet don't have the hands-on experience on your résumé. This means that you have *some* of the experience or tangential experience needed to accomplish the task, but you've never taken on a task exactly like the one you're going after. Therefore, you're going to have to prove that you have confidence in yourself to get the task done. You aren't trying to fool anyone; you're simply representing your hand as strongly as possible.

If you believe the company or person you are pitching to isn't living up to their potential, and you believe you can help them to improve, then it is the right time to semibluff in order to seal the deal. So many times in my life, I've known in my heart that I was ready to take on a big task or take that next step in my career, but my résumé just didn't support me enough to make it obvious to others. In those situations I have used semibluffing to help convince whomever needed convincing that I was the right man for the job.

It's important to keep in mind that I've semibluffed only when I honestly believed I was the best person for that given task or job. Of course, there have been a few times in my career when I haven't lived up to the hand I represented, but for the most part the people who have bet on me throughout my life have made the right choice. A semibluff is never a guaranteed win. Sometimes you're going to lose, but that's no reason not to semibluff. You're going to have to believe in yourself with every fiber of your being if you're going to convince anyone you're worth a damn in this world. And if you want to keep moving on to levels in your career in which you've never worked before, you're going to have to semibluff to get there.

Anytime you have full confidence in your abilities and are faced with an opportunity to make a leap in your career, win a project, close a deal, or land a new job, that is the correct time to semibluff.

No one's going to think less of you for bluffing them out of all their chips at a poker table. They may hate you, but they won't think less of you. In poker, bluffing is a part of the game—but it's different in business. In business, people's livelihoods are at stake. People's welfare, their families, and their futures are on the line in the business world. While this book can teach you to turn your job into a game and have more fun and achieve greater success in your career, it's not advocating that you apply the same ethics to your business life that you apply to your poker game. While poker is a great battleground in which to learn how to effectively semibluff in the business world, don't let the bluffing get out of control and seep into your career.

THE SHOWDOWN

In poker, bluff whenever you can—but don't create
a bad table image by stealing too many pots.
In business, semibluff whenever you need to—but
make sure you're confident in your abilities, and
never take on more than you can handle.

KNOW WHEN YOU'RE BEAT
The Tragedy of Pairing

In chapter 5 ("Make the Most Out of a Great Hand"), we covered how to maximize your wins with an extremely strong hand. In this chapter, we're going to learn how to minimize your losses with a good hand.

Sound strange?

Why would anyone need to minimize their losses with a *good* hand? Shouldn't you be taking down big pots on a good hand? Well sure, taking down big pots is always your main objective, but think of it this way: you rarely lose all your money on a hand like 8-7s (the *s* stands for suited—both cards being of the same suit); you lose all your money on hands like pocket jacks. Let me explain.

If you enter a hand with 8-7s (the full importance of which

we'll cover in the next chapter) and you don't hit top pair, two pairs, trips, or an open-ended straight draw, it makes it very easy for you to lay down the hand. No questions asked. A pair of pocket jacks, on the other hand, can be a lot harder for most players to lay down. For the average or beginning poker player, knowing when to fold a hand like pocket jacks can be very confusing and rather difficult. Some players get so excited when they look under their hole cards to find two matching cards staring back at them that they completely lose their grasp on reality and hardly notice that they're drawing dead on the flop. Too many exciting poker showdowns on television and too many bad poker scenes in western films have tricked the modern poker player into overestimating the true power of the pocket pair.

An even more common occurrence is a player hitting top pair on the flop and thinking he or she has got it made. Maybe you made a large bet and entered the pot with A-Ks. The flop comes K, Q, 9. All you see is that you've got top pair with a big kicker. You get so excited that your hands practically shake as you reach back for your chips, imagining how much you're going to win on this hand. You hardly even take a moment to think that your opponent might have you beat with J-10s, trip nines, or even worse—maybe he made a flush on the flop. You end up going all in with your top pair, and you lose your whole stack in the process. You thought you had the nuts, but all you had was a high pair.

This, at its essence, is the *tragedy of pairing*.

Knowing when to lay day down a *good* hand when there is strong evidence that one of your opponents may be holding a *great* hand is a necessary lesson to learn in your journey to becoming a strong, agile player. After all, it's not the bad hands you lose money on, and it's rarely the great hands you lose money on either. Most of the time you lose your chips on the *good* hands—the hands that are strong enough to cause you to bet, but not strong enough to take down the pot.

Some times in business, knowing when you're about to take a loss is instinctual. Sometimes you get a gut feeling a deal is about to go sour and you pull out before it all falls apart. Sometimes it's just blind luck that you get out of the way of a bad deal before it pulls you down with it. Yet, if you relied on luck for every deal in your business life, you would probably find yourself jobless and penniless in no time. Knowing what signs to look for and what to be aware of when entering a deal, expecting a promotion, or even starting a new business, can often be the difference between walking away unscathed and having the roof cave in on top of you. Knowing when you're beat is all about recognizing the moment a *good* hand becomes a losing hand, and having the strength to lay it down.

In this chapter, I'll cover the necessary process one must go through when deciding the right time to lay down a strong hand. Knowing when you're beat is an essential step in protecting your stack and surviving to see another hand.

Unless one has the total nuts, no one knows for sure when they're going to win a hand. Having the full and total nuts is also the only time you can know for sure that you're not going to lose the hand. Play anything outside of the nuts and you're going to be doing a bit of gambling—no matter how strong your hand is. Being a smart player, both in business and in poker, is about gambling intelligently by having the most information behind each of your decisions. Playing wisely is about minimizing your losses.

We should be glad that there is gambling involved in the game—it's something to celebrate, not bemoan. After all, if there were no gambling or risk taking involved, it would be impossible to win at poker or in business without having the best hand. If it weren't for strategy, the path of your career would be as random and arbitrary as the flip of a coin. On the other hand, employing a strategy means taking a risk.

For the most part, this chapter is about risk assessment. It's about figuring out if a hand is actually strong enough to continue playing. Most decisions you will make at the poker table or at the office will be difficult ones. The best hands and the worst hands are easy to play. These are also the hands that you play less frequently, since you rarely play bad hands and the great hands don't come along very often. As long as you're not playing wildly, the majority of the hands you play will be merely good. Therefore, few things are more important than assessing the risk involved in your hand before deciding whether to stay in or muck it and walk away.

In chapter 5 we discussed the importance of knocking your opponents out of the hand as quickly as possible when the pot is large and when you believe your hand is the best. The only way to knock other players out of a hand is to make a large bet. If your bet is large enough, it will make it too expensive for the straight draws and the flush draws to continue in the hand. The medium or small pairs will assume they're beat and fold as well. If you get called, you're either beaten by a better hand or you're about to win a large pot. This is why you only attempt to win a large pot right then and there with the best of hands, the near nuts. To make a bet large enough to scare out the rest of the players and then *to lose the hand* would make this play too risky to attempt with anything outside of the strongest of hands.

With the more mediocre hands you don't have the option of taking the easy way out by making a large, decisive bet and forcing your opponents to a decision (when I refer to your hand, I'm not referring to your hole cards, I'm referring to your five-card hand).

Whether you're on the flop, the turn, or the river, without a very strong hand your risk of getting called and getting beat is too great to make a large bet. Therefore, playing these mediocre hands can get a bit tricky.

I've found that there are four steps every player should take when assessing the risk of playing a hand:

1. Never assume

2. Make a read

3. Probe for information

4. Make a decision

This process is a fail-safe to help prevent you from stepping into a big loss unknowingly. In the following pages, I will walk you through this process while showing you the application of each point in both the business and the poker worlds. The process is easy, it makes sense, and it works. If you put all of your good hands under the scrutiny of this process, you will effectively minimize your losses and, in turn, maximize your wins.

NEVER ASSUME

This one is easy, yet it is commonly forgotten. Unless you've figured out that you have the complete nuts, there is always a hand out there that can beat you. There is always a chance, no matter how slim, that you will be playing against someone who has the exact hand needed to beat yours. If your opponent doesn't have a hand that can beat yours, there's a chance that on the turn or on the river your opponent will make a hand strong enough to beat yours. As obvious as it may sound, remember this: unless you have the total and complete nuts, there is a chance your opponent has you beat or will have you beat at the showdown.

Players often get drunk on their hand—they become so enamored with their hand that they forget that there's a possibility they could still lose. This especially happens during a long streak of bad hands. Let's say you've been folding hands all night long. You haven't seen a playable hand in an hour and a half. It happens. Sometimes the cards run cold. You finally get a nice little A-Qs. You're one of the first to act, and you make a medium-sized raise to scare out the small pockets and the A-xs (ace and a card lower than ten) and head into the pot with two other players. The flop comes A, 9, 8 rainbow (meaning three different suits).

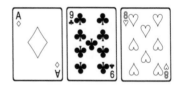

THE FLOP

YOU   OPPONENT

You've got a pair of aces with a strong kicker on the flop.

You've got top pair and a nice kicker. "Finally," you say to yourself, "a winning hand." You make a medium bet and get called. The turn comes a ten. Now you've got top pair and a straight draw. You make another medium-sized bet and you get raised. A big raise.

Without even thinking you go all in, assuming this guy is trying to push you around. He turns over his cards to show the 9-8s. The river comes a rag (a low card), and you lose the pot. Your opponent had two pairs on the flop, and you never even saw it coming.

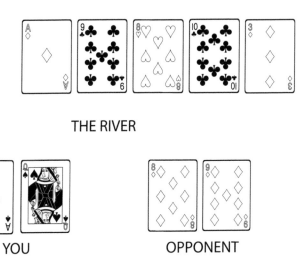

THE RIVER

YOU   OPPONENT

Unfortunately, he had you beat the whole time.

It's not like there was nothing you could do. For the most part, you played the hand incorrectly. Your opponent gave you plenty of clues. If you had been more aware and taken yourself through the four steps, you would have seen them and you would have appropriately folded your hand. You'll find out what those clues were in the following steps.

Just as looking down and seeing two great hole cards can intoxicate a player and cause him to play poorly, so can an excellent idea or a great deal in the business world. In fact, it happens with start-ups all the time. They come up with an exciting, innovative idea or product. They have no problem getting a ton of investment money—there is great industry buzz about what they're working on. They get great press. They put together a crack team of the best minds in the industry, and the next thing they know their company tanks and they all go bankrupt. During the e-boom of the mid-to-late 1990s, this was almost a weekly occurrence.

The start-up heads became so enamored with their own potential and with their own initial success that they completely failed to see the clues that basic common sense would have made apparent. In the following steps, I will cover just what clues can help you to decide whether or not your business plan has the potential of blowing up in your faces.

Even within your own career you might assume you're in a great position, yet lose perspective on the reality of the situation. You can never assume, even the day after a promotion, that you are truly protected within your company. Even contracts can be broken. I'm not telling you to walk around in a state of paranoia—far from it. I'm simply reminding you of the importance of always staying aware. Never assume everything is perfect.

As I said at the start of this section, assuming your hand is infallible is the first step to taking a big, unexpected loss. Always remember that unless you have the complete and total nuts, there is always a hand or a card out there than can beat whatever hand you're holding. Never assume you've got the best hand until you've followed the next three steps, and even then, there's always a chance you will lose. That's why it's called *gambling*.

MAKE A READ

Do your best to make a solid read on your opponent. This is a big one. If you could accurately and consistently read your opponent's hand, you would never make an incorrect decision. While there's always the possibility of reading your opponent correctly and *still* losing the hand because your opponent catches a miracle card on the river, you would at least always be making statistically correct plays if you were able to read your opponent's hand.

There are many ways to read an opponent's hand. I'm not going to get into physical tells here because there are just too many to cover, and people in general are far too diverse in their tells to make any discussion of it worthwhile. If you're still interested in tells, the best book on the subject is and probably always will be *Caro's Book of Poker Tells: The Psychology and Body Language of Poker* by Mike Caro (New York: Cardoza, 2003).

To me, the most effective tells, and the ones that translate best into the world of business, are the tells that come from a person's actions. Keeping track of how a player has acted in the past, both in the game as a whole and in the actions he or she has taken in the current hand, always adds up to a good deal of information that can be used to help gauge the next step. By watching how a particular player plays throughout a game, you can learn a lot about their playing style. Have they been bluffing often? What types of hands do they like to play? Are they tight? Are they loose? Do they bet aggressively when they have a weak hand, or vice versa?

In the actual hand, it is important to notice how a player has played his or her hand up until the present moment. Did your opponent limp in? Did he or she make a large raise? If your opponent called, did he call quickly or did he think about it for a moment? How did your opponent play his hand on the flop? Judging from his or her actions, do you believe the flop helped or hurt your opponent's hand?

By asking yourself these questions and keeping track of your opponent's actions, you'll be able to get a solid read on how your opponent plays the game. A player gives away a ton of information in the way he or she actually plays the game, and usually it's enough to make an educated guess.

When you've got a good hand and your opponent makes a large reraise—a raise large enough to represent a very strong hand—the question you've got to ask yourself is whether you believe your opponent is bluffing or not. This is the question I always get stuck on. I hate getting bluffed or bullied out of a pot. I hate having top pair and a great kicker and worrying that some jerk with nothing is trying to bully me out of a hand. My distaste for getting bullied out a hand often causes me to call purely just to find out if my opponent is bluffing. This is usually a bad move. There's no need to leave the fate of your cards up to such a random decision. There are ways to get a better read on your opponent and gain a chance to decipher whether or not he or she is in fact bluffing.

Let's get back to the hand we spoke of in step 1 where you lost with a pair of aces. What clues did your opponent give you that he indeed had a better hand than you? What clues did your opponent give you that he wasn't bluffing?

You made a medium-sized preflop bet with your A-Qs and got two callers. You were in an early position, meaning close to the button and therefore one of the first people to act in the hand, and you were first to raise the pot. One of your callers was a few positions ahead of you, and the player who eventually beat you in the hand was sitting on the button. Your medium-sized bet was not necessarily an incorrect move, considering your early position. Some players may simply call with A-Qs in early position and wait to see how the rest of the table acts. Making a large bet is a mistake, since anyone who calls you most likely has you beat—and you don't want that. A medium-sized bet is smart. If you get callers, you're in a good position; if you get raised, you'll have a good opportunity to fold the hand without losing too many chips.

Just by thinking about how your opponents played preflop and noticing where they were sitting at the table should give you a good amount of information. The player who called you in early position most likely has a decent hand, either a middle pocket pair or a high connector (two sequential face cards). There's a chance your opponent has queens, kings, or A-Ks, yet most players with those hands would reraise in this situation to keep the pot heads-up. Most likely his hand is in the good category, just like yours. On the other hand, your opponent on the button could almost have anything. Because the button is such an advantageous position, most players will play a wider variety of hands in that position. Considering that your bet was only of a medium size, it's very possible your opponent could have a low pair or a small suited connector (like the 9-8, which he ends up beating you with in the end). The fact that your opponent called on the button should tell you that he could have any hand in the decent to great categories. Put simply: at this point in the hand, you have no idea what this guy is holding. He's a wild card.

The flop comes A, 8, 9 rainbow, meaning three different suits. Because you have top pair and a high kicker (a pair of aces with a queen kicker), you believe you have a very strong hand. You may not necessarily be wrong (at this point in the hand you might be right) but you really haven't been given enough information by the other players to warrant excitement. Thinking your hand is strong, you decide to make another medium-sized bet. You want callers. You want more money in this pot. Without even really thinking about it, you've decided to slow-play your competition. Is this a smart move? Not at all.

Remember back to our chapter on slow-playing: you never slow-play unless you've got an *extremely strong hand*. The player closest to you folds his hand. He most likely had a small pair and doesn't like the ace on the flop, or possibly he had a high connector and didn't hit anything. He made a good fold. The player on the button quickly and calmly calls. This action should make you think: why would someone call? There are only three reasons your opponent would call:

1. You opponent has a good hand but wants more information about your hand before he raises.

2. Your opponent is on a draw and, considering the odds, thinks your bet is small enough to warrant a call.

3. Your opponent has a great hand and he's slow-playing you.

No matter which one is true, his call should be a warning to you.

The turn comes a ten and you make yet *another* medium-sized bet. This is a major mistake. Your constant medium-sized bets serve no purpose since they give you little to no information on your opponent's hand. If he calls, you have gained no information because his hand may be weak but the pot odds still warrant a call, and if he raises you, you still have no information since he may have sensed weakness and decided to try and bluff you out.

Your opponent quickly raises your medium-sized bet, and you—fed up with his reraising and drunk on the power of your hand—reraise him all in. Why would your opponent reraise you? Two reasons: either he has you beat or he's bluffing. While it's possible that he may be bluffing, most likely he isn't, considering his betting patterns in this hand and the card that came on the turn. Your opponent's reaction to the turn card's being a ten should tell you all you need to know to get out of the hand. Because there's a serious straight draw on the table, your opponent needed to make it far too expensive for you to continue in the hand if, in fact, you were still on a draw. You have to figure that he guessed you had an ace in your hand because of the way you bet on the flop. Assuming you have an ace and a high card, and seeing the 8, 9, 10 on the table, he wanted to protect his two pairs to the best of his ability by doing whatever he could to stop you from making a straight. Your impulsive all-in call left him no choice but to call you—the pot odds were too good. And anyway, he had put you on a pair of aces since the flop and still believed his two pairs were the best.

By carefully watching your opponent's betting actions and reactions you would have learned almost everything you needed to know to figure out the right move. The only thing you were missing was your read on whether or not your opponent was bluffing, which we'll cover in the next step.

In the business world, your opponent's actions are just as necessary to notice as they are at the poker table, yet in the world of business there are many more factors a good player must take notice of in order to stay aware. There are dozens of reasons a start-up company can fall apart. Maybe they haven't identified their market, or they haven't obtained enough capital. Your start-up might have an amazing product that the whole industry is excited about, yet some kid in his garage happens to make a similar product that's cheaper and more user friendly and all of a sudden your entire company falls apart. Another point to consider is that your start-up company's team may look great on paper, but there's a chance that team may not work well together in reality. Just as in poker, pocket aces look great on paper, but when there's a flush draw on the table, those aces lose a lot of their value.

In order to never get caught holding a losing hand you believed to be strong, you must stay fully aware of your industry. You've got to do a thorough investigation of your market. Know what's available, know what's out there, track your competition regularly, the big guys and the small guys. Even though it may be basic, staying aware of your industry and your competition is utterly important to understanding the true strength of your product and/or your organization.

The reason so many start-ups failed during the e-boom was the acceleration of business. Everyone wanted to get their company up and running as quickly as possible. Everyone rushed to get their products on the market before they became outdated. The speed at which people played their hands was almost as fast as hands are actually played at the poker table. If they had only slowed down a bit and taken more time to make sure their businesses were aware of the competition and the market, a lot more of those e-businesses would have folded their hands before they had them folded for them.

On the more personal side of the business world, imagine you were just promoted to a new position, but now you have a new boss. Take the time to learn how this new boss conducts business before you make any big moves. Be aware of how your new colleagues and peers act in relation to the boss. Having a new boss can be a very negative thing, especially if your last boss was better at seeing your vision. Yet most people don't like to take the time to think about these things. They want to continue on with a business-as-usual attitude whenever they feel they're holding a strong hand. If anything, be more cautious of the strong hands simply because those are the moments when you may have the tendency to fall asleep at the wheel.

PROBE FOR INFORMATION

The more information you have, the better your chances will be of correctly reading your opponent and making the right call. While the previous step covered how to gather information by carefully observing your opponent's actions, this step is all about taking actions that will force your opponent to give up valuable information.

At the poker table, the best way to probe for information is to make a bet. Checking gives you very little information (unless your opponent checks as well) since a check might cause your opponent to sense weakness and to bet regardless of his or her cards. Making a small to medium-sized bet gives you little information as well, since your opponent may feel the pot odds justify a call even if his hand is weak. Therefore the only way to gain any information is to make a nice, big bet.

A nice, big bet will put your opponent to a decision. He had better have a very good hand (or be just plain crazy) to call your bet. Nothing will shut down a bluff like an extremely large bet. At the same time, you had better be pretty damn confident in the strength of your hand, or in your opponent's bluff, in order to put so many chips on the line. If your opponent calls you, you know he has a strong hand. How strong his hand is can be determined only by making a read on his overall playing style and the way he has played this particular hand. But if he calls, you know for sure he's got a strong hand. It's up to you to make an appropriate read at that point.

At what point in the hand you make a large decision-forcing bet is very important as well. The right time to make such a bet is when you feel that you have no idea what your opponent may have in his hand, or you're trying to call out his bluff. When you know your medium-sized bets are going to get called and your checks are going to get raised, it's time to either give up the hand by checking and folding when your opponent bets or make a large bet. Those are your only options.

In our example hand, you would make a large bet after the flop. You got cold-called by the button preflop, which means he could have had any kind of hand, but most likely a hand on the weaker side of the spectrum because of his strong table position. You had top pair and a strong kicker, so the only way you could have found out if someone had a *very* strong hand was to make a large enough bet to put your opponent to a decision. And yet, making a decision-forcing bet would have been the *wrong* move for that particular hand—and not just because we know the outcome of the hand. The reason a large bet would have been the wrong decision in that hand is that you are in a weak position.

Being in an early position on the table puts you at a decided disadvantage to the rest of the table. To put up a large bet with two players ahead of you—two players whose hands you have almost no read on—is too risky. Because of your position, you are really stuck with only two options: a medium-sized bet or a check. Since checking is very rarely the right move because it has no chance of winning the pot right there and then, a medium-sized bet is really your only play. Your medium-sized bet causes one player to fold and one player to call. You still haven't learned anything about the player on the button. On the turn you really have no good options either, since a very large bet might get called and a check will surely get raised. Because of the lack of power in your position, the right move here is to either check and fold or to make a medium-sized bet and fold if your opponent reraises. I would probably make a medium-sized bet and either try to win it right there or fold when I get raised. At this point in the hand, I would be so wary of my position that I wouldn't feel too confident in my pair of aces, especially since there's a straight draw on the table.

In this particular example hand, there is very little information you can get, purely because of your position. It's important to realize that probing for information is often possible only if you're in a strong position. In the business world, it works exactly the same.

Probing for information within your market or industry is a lot easier if you're a company with a large stack. If your company has made a strong name for itself, it is a lot easier to test a new product before you enter the market with it. People will be more lenient with an established name brand or a company with a strong track record behind it. If you're a small company with a small stack, you risk your entire company's reputation with every product you reveal and every move you make, making product testing and other forms of information gathering very difficult.

If you're in a new job or suddenly find yourself with what you consider to be a strong hand, often the best way to learn the true strength of your position is to be straight with your boss. Ask how strong your position really is, how much leeway you have to make a few moves. Talk to your colleagues to get a better feel for the mood within your company. Once again, if you're not in a good position, it might not be the right time to go probing for information. People may be inclined to only tell you as much as they want you to know.

Try making a few moves and see how much you can get done without ruffling anyone's feathers. Try to set up some deals or land a few new accounts. Just as in poker, the best way to find out the strength of your hand or get a better read on your opponent's hand is to make a large bet. As long as you believe in the strength of your hand and you're in a good position, probing for information by taking action is often the best way to ensure that you don't get caught holding a bad hand. But remember, if you're out of position and feel as though you can't get anything done within your company, or are unable to get a feel for where you stand within your company, it's time to reevaluate your hand and possibly even get prepared to fold your hand.

MAKE A DECISION

When push comes to shove, you have to act. The first three steps should give you all the information you need to make the most educated move possible. If you've taken in as much information as possible and still don't know exactly what to do, well, that's all a part of the game. There's always a bit of gambling involved. All you can do is try to make the best possible decision and hope it's the right one. I think you'll find that the better you get at walking yourself through the four steps, the stronger your intuition will be and the more instinctual these types of plays will become.

In 1998 I became involved in a classic tragedy of pairing situation. I had just left EA (Electronic Arts) and was looking to start up my own video game company in China. Because of my experience with video games in China, I had a good deal of interest from game publishers and investors looking to get involved in whatever I was going to do next in the Chinese video game market. It was around this time that a few friends of mine came to me with an idea for a startup company that eventually came to be known as Muse.

The idea for Muse excited me. The goal was to produce software designed to allow entertainment content services for broadband Internet. While the product Muse produced is a bit technical and complicated to explain, it was a company I felt had broad, far-reaching implications. I believed that Muse had a great deal of potential in a relatively untapped market. The problem was that Muse was about ten years ahead of the curve.

Muse was partially under way when I was brought on to get it up and going. I felt passionately about the idea. Even though the video game company I was planning on starting in China had a lot of potential, I felt as though Muse had more. Muse looked like pocket aces to me. The moment I joined Muse I was able to raise a good chunk of investment money. It seemed as though everything was going perfectly. When I first came on board, Muse felt like an extremely strong hand.

Over the next few months we started to notice a lack of interest in our product by the Internet service providers—the people we needed most to champion our technology. In addition, the investment money we believed we were getting didn't come through all at once. Slowly, Muse started to take a turn for the worse, but I stuck it out, hoping to weather the storm.

I ignored the signs, attempting to struggle through them as opposed to realizing that I was playing a losing hand and folding appropriately. Although the idea for Muse was strong, the market wasn't ready and the timing wasn't right. I had pocket aces but I never realized that there were four flush cards on the table—and I wasn't holding any cards in that suit.

While taking big risks, like the risk of joining Muse, is an integral part of being a successful businessperson, I failed to notice the signs that Muse was not going to succeed. I failed to fold when I should have folded. I became intoxicated by how strong I believed the hand to be and lost sight of the reality of the situation. If I had paid a little more attention to the signs, I could have probably gotten out of the hand in time to go back and start up a video game company in China, which most likely would have been an easier and better hand to play.

The tragedy of pairing has happened to all of us. It's hard to constantly be thinking about how strong your hand actually is once you believe you've finally landed one. In business, it's hard not to get caught up in the excitement of rumors of a promotion or a good deal or a strong business model. But unless the hand is *great*, it's important to take a moment before you act and walk yourself through the four steps to help you figure out how strong your hand really is.

Remember, you don't want your boss or your opponent at the card table to take control of your hand and make your decision for you. You want to retain as much control of your hand as possible at all times. By getting caught up in what seems to be such a good thing, you basically hand over the reins to your opponent and take a backseat to the action. Unless you have the complete nuts you never have a sure thing. You always have to watch your hand and your opponents.

To become a great poker player you have to learn to fold trip aces when you believe your opponent has a flush. To become a great businessperson you have to be able to walk away from a strong deal when you think the timing just isn't right. You have to be able to take a step back from the poker table or the boardroom and see the situation objectively. If you were watching your hand from a distance, with no attachment to winning or losing, would you still play your aces strongly if your opponent played back at you aggressively? Or would you slow down for a minute and try and get a solid read on your opponent before blindly tossing chips towards the middle.

There's nothing worse than going all in and losing to a hand you didn't even see coming. You've got to always have a read on your opponent. You must always at least put him on a hand—meaning you have a solid guess as to the cards in your opponent's hands. Your guesses may often be wrong, but if you aren't making educated guesses you're just flying blind.

THE SHOWDOWN

It's not the *worst* hands or the *best* hands you have to be wary of—it's the GOOD hands. Pay extra attention to the *good* hands—never assume you have the winning hand.

ALWAYS KEEP THEM GUESSING
Small Suited Connectors

I'm playing a home tournament No-Limit Hold 'Em game with a few of my coworkers. There's a $50 buy-in and everyone gets $5,000 in chips. The player with all the chips at the end of the night wins all of the buy-in money. The game is friendly, but we're all pretty competitive and no one wants to walk away a loser. We're a few hours into the game when I come across what I consider to be the most important hand in all of poker: the small suited connector. Why do I consider it so? Well, the best way to show the power of the small suited connector is simply to show you how the hand played out.

The button deals out hole cards to the nine sitting players. I'm in middle position. I've been playing aggressively all night, but I'm not the bully at the table. I've been taking down a bunch of small to medium-sized pots and betting aggressively. So far it's paid off, making me the big stack at the table by about a two-to-one chip count.

The player to my right looks at his cards, takes a deep breath, and counts out a few hundred in chips. I watch him do the math in his head. He wants to make a decent-sized bet but doesn't want to scare everyone out. He drops $500 in chips in the pot, about four times the size of the big blind. This is a bet that wants a call. I put him on a big pair, probably kings.

I could put this guy all in, lose the pot, and still be the chip leader, but that's no reason to call. I check my cards and find my very favorite hand in all of No-Limit Hold 'Em: the 6-7 ♦, or what's referred to as a small suited connector.

I feel extremely confident playing hands like 6-7 suited. In fact, I'd take hands like these over a traditionally big hand like A-K any day of the week. Why? Because with small suited connectors you either win a big pot or only lose a small one. It's exactly the type of risk you want to be taking at the poker table. If you don't hit anything on the flop and someone bets into you, then you just fold the hand. No questions asked, easy decision. But if you do hit something, say two pairs, trips, a straight or a flush draw, then you've got a good shot at taking down a big pot. On top of that, no one at the table could have a clue as to what cards you're holding.

If I raised he'd most likely try and push me all in and 6-7s definitely isn't a great all-in hand. Remember, it's the type of hand you either win a big pot with or lose a small one with, not the type of hand you put everything on the line with before the flop.

I call his bet. The blinds fold and the dealer burns and turns the next three cards. I couldn't ask for a better flop: 5 ♦, 4 ♦, and 6 ♣. I've got a mountain of outs. Any diamond gives me a flush, a three or an eight makes me a straight, I've got top pair with a shot at making a set of sixes, and I've even got a very small chance of hitting the miracle straight flush.

Since he's to my right, he gets to bet first. He comes in with a bet of $1,000, double what he bet before. He's trying to chase me off the draw, whether it be a straight draw or a flush draw. Usually, if I didn't have so many outs, a bet like that would be enough to stop me from drawing and to lay down my hand, but with my chip position and the mountain of outs I have in front of me, there isn't a bet he could make that I wouldn't call—and I still have him on pocket kings.

I push all in. It's time to gamble.

Before I have time to take my hands off my chips, he pushes his chips toward the middle and flips over his cards. Pocket queens. I was close. Luckily, neither of them is a diamond. I flip my cards. He scowls. He knows how many outs I have.

"No diamond," he says. The dealer turns the next two cards. The J ♥ comes first. No help to either of us. I'm calm. I've still got close to 16 cards that could come to make my hand. Dealer turns the next card: A ♦.

I made my flush.

The former owner of two queens grunts in frustration and I take down a big pot.

That's the beauty of the small suited connector. No one sees it coming and you have to take only a marginal risk in comparison to the big money at stake in the pot. The small suited connector is truly one of the great secrets to winning large pots and making big moves in No-Limit Hold 'Em.

In this chapter, I will teach you one of the most important secrets for succeeding in business and poker. In this chapter, you'll learn how to win the huge pots, risk only the small ones, and come out looking like a hero. Let's start with the poker side of small suited connectors and work our way up to applying this secret sauce to the business world.

A BRIEF EXPLANATION OF THE SMALL SUITED CONNECTOR

The phrase *small suited connector* simply means any low hole cards that are connected numerically (4-5, 5-6, 6-7, etc.) and suited, meaning both hole cards are of the same suit. When I say small suited connectors, I'm referring only to the 6-7s (remember, *s* means suited), 7-8s, and 8-9s. The 2-3s, 3-4s, and 4-5s could be considered small suited connectors as well, but because of their lower numbers, statistically speaking, they don't hold up in play as strongly as the 6-7s, 7-8s, or the 8-9s; therefore, I don't recommend them to be used in the manner explained in this chapter.

That goes double for the A-2s and the 9-10s, which on their own can often be decent hands to play, but not if you're going to try and play them as small suited connectors. Unless you're heads up with just one other player, A-2s can be a pretty worthless hand to play. What happens if an ace comes on the flop and there's a handful of other players in the hand with you? You may have top pair but you've also got the weakest kicker, making your hand nearly worthless since you've got to figure at least one other player is holding an ace. Even if you land the straight, you can get beaten out by a six-high straight. With A-2 you're either looking for heads-up play (thus increasing your chances of being the only player in the hand with an ace) or, because your cards are suited, you're looking for the ace-high flush.

Same with the 9-10s: even if you land the straight, you still have a good chance of losing the hand to someone with a jack-high or even ace-high straight. When you start playing with cards as high as 9-10s, you have a higher chance of being in the straight draw with players who hold much better straight drawing cards than you. Since most players play with at least one face card in their hand, having 9-10s is almost the same as having two very low face cards. The 9-10s is not quite high enough to beat the majority of hands you're likely to play against, and they're not quite low enough to deceive anyone by staying under the radar the way a hand like 6-7s can. Put simply, attempt the small suited connector technique only with the 6-7s, 7-8s, or 8-9s.

A lot of players will tell you that suited cards are overrated since the chances of hitting a flush are slim in comparison to the chances of hitting top pair, two pairs, trips, or a straight, and generally I would agree: most players do overvalue the suited cards. A-Ks isn't made that much stronger by having both of them suited, but when it comes to small cards, like 6-7, having them suited can make a big difference. When you're playing suited connectors, you're not playing to land the small hands; you're playing to land or draw to the strong hands—such as trips, straights, and flushes—so any edge you can get, such as having the cards be suited, is necessary in order to play the small suited connector effectively.

PLAYING THE SMALL SUITED CONNECTOR AT THE POKER TABLE

Playing the small suited connector is as simple as can be, which is part of its beauty. When you find yourself dealt one of these hands, be willing to call a medium-sized bet, maybe setting the ceiling at 20 percent of your total chip stack. Anything higher than that and

♠

the risk will outweigh your statistical chances of winning. It's better to be the caller than the raiser with small suited connectors, since calling will better conceal the strength of your hand. If no one bothers to raise the hand by the time it comes to you, make a medium-sized bet to get some money in the pot, but don't scare out the playing field. When it comes to small suited connectors, the more people in the hand, the better.

When the flop comes, you're not just looking for a very strong hand; you're looking for a ton of outs to a very strong hand. You're looking for top two pairs, trips, a straight, a flush, or better. Having just top pair in this situation is nearly worthless, since almost any pocket pair will usually have you beaten (as we saw in the example from my friendly coworker game), so if you're going to land something on the flop, it had better be strong if you're going to continue in the hand.

If you don't land a very strong hand on the flush, you're hoping you have enough outs to make a bet or a call worthwhile. Just as in my friendly coworker game, I had a ton of outs. I'm no statistician but I think my friend and I were statistically pretty close, with my friend with pocket queens having me beaten by maybe 10 percent. Even though I was the underdog, I had a bunch of ways to win: two pairs, trips, straights, flushes, and even a straight flush. The only way he could improve his hand would have been by landing another queen or both queens—both statistical long shots. Granted, if I hadn't made a stronger hand by landing one of my outs on the river, I would have been dead in the water, but I took a chance and felt my hand was strong enough to gamble on. It helped that even if I had lost the hand I still would have had a big stack of chips in front of me. There's even a good chance I wouldn't have gone all in if the tables were turned and I were the one with the small stack, but I would have thought long and hard about it and the gambler in me would like to think that I would have called it regardless.

HOW I PLAY THE SMALL SUITED CONNECTOR

I play small suited connectors as follows: if I have a small stack, I play the hand only if I make a strong hand on the flop. If I have a big stack, I'll probably play the hand as long as I have a few good outs after the flop. If I have neither of those things, I'll fold the hand no matter what the size of my stack. Whenever you play the small suited connector, you're hoping someone has a strong hand against you, usually pocket pair or top pair. You want a flop with a high card and then a bunch of low cards (hopefully low cards that make you two pairs, trips, a straight, or a flush). The best-case scenario is that your opponent lands top pair, isn't scared off by the low cards on the flop, and bets into you big for the next few betting rounds. You can slow-play a bit to get the pot bigger, but it doesn't really matter. If your opponent has a strong hand and sees nothing but small cards on the table, he most likely won't assume you're playing with small cards (since most players don't) and will therefore bet into you courageously. This is exactly how small suited connectors pay off.

A quick word on landing the flush with the small suited connector: Because your cards are low, a flush can be a dangerous thing with small suited connectors. Most likely, if another player has also made a flush at the table, he or she has you beaten. With small suited connectors, the more flush cards on the table, the weaker your hand. Your best hope is to land the flush on the flop. You want to make a big bet to chase out anyone drawing to a bigger flush and hopefully take the pot down right then and there. If there are four flush cards on the table (four community cards of the same suit), most likely you're beaten, unless you're playing heads up. Just remember, the more flush cards on the table, the weaker your small suited connector flush probably is.

That, for the most part, is how you play the small suited connector at the poker table. It's a great way to pull down huge pots, make big moves in tournaments, and keep your competition on its toes. The great thing about the small suited connector is that it teaches your opponents that you are a danger with just about any two cards in your hand. Not only can you win large pots with the big hands like A-K, but you also win large pots with commonly considered weak hands like 6-7s. Now that you know the true power of 6-7s, you know better than to consider them weak. You know they're one of the great secrets to winning in No-Limit Hold 'Em.

One of the most amazing things I've found during my life as a poker player and a businessman is that the small suited connector is just as effective and powerful a secret weapon in the business world as it is at the poker table. Let's see how.

THE SMALL SUITED CONNECTOR IN BUSINESS

Truly, if there is a secret sauce to my career, it is the small suited connector. If there is one trick that has helped get me where I am today, it is my ability to consistently find ways to parlay my natural playing style and my skill set into a new division or market for the companies I've worked for. You always want your coworkers, your bosses, and your industry asking themselves, "What's this person going to do next?" The small suited connector is how I keep everyone around me guessing.

Used correctly, the small suited connector is a great way to make a major move in your career. Put simply, the small suited connector is a great way to keep an eye out for opportunities that, because of your specific skill sets and talents, you and only you have the potential of taking advantage of. Slow and steady doesn't always win the race, especially in today's fast-track global market. Taking your industry by surprise with an out-of-the-box idea is often the only way to achieve great success. The small suited connector gives you the chance to move ahead quickly in your career without the risk usually associated with new, untested products or ideas.

You can't simply walk into your boss's office one day and demand to take over a major division of the company. Instead, you've got to take your boss by surprise with an idea never attempted before at your company. The idea alone has to get your boss's attention and inspire him or her to create an entirely new division for you to run. Much like we discussed in chapter 5, you have to slow-play a great idea in order for it to fully pay off, and small suited connectors are the path to coming up with those great ideas.

In this chapter, I'll get into the details of how you can implement small suited connectors in your career by putting all the little pieces together in order to make one big move.

Sure, you could go to Harvard, get an MBA, and land a great job at Procter & Gamble. In the poker world, a career like that would be considered pocket aces—a huge hand. With a career like that, no one could ever say you didn't have an extremely strong hand in the business world. But it's also possible to achieve that kind of success with a hand no one in the business world expects you to play, a hand no one sees coming. It is possible to find great success and win the big pots with the business equivalent of a 6-7s. To me, the small suited connector isn't just a good way to make a big move in your career, it is hands down the best way. It's the only way to win the huge pots while risking only the small ones.

Enough talk. Here's how you do it.

HOW TO TAKE ADVANTAGE OF THE SMALL SUITED CONNECTORS IN BUSINESS

The majority of the truly successful men and women of the business world didn't get to where they are today by putting in a consistent, long-term effort. The way these people moved ahead in their careers was by finding an opportunity and taking advantage of it before the opportunity had become obvious to everyone else. Not to say that many of the world's most successful businessmen and -women aren't hard workers with great skills and talents—of course they are—but they didn't achieve their success on perseverance alone.

Many of today's most successful entrepreneurs achieved their success by following through with an idea ahead of its time, by having the vision to recognize the potential of a new idea and to make it happen. This is half of the key to making a big jump in your career: you've got to follow through with all of your ideas. The other half is the process of taking all of your connections and putting them together to help get your opportunity off the ground. By combining your connections and involving others you make taking on large, new projects practically risk free.

In business, a correctly executed small suited connector is a combination of following through with your ideas and putting all the pieces together. By doing so, you'll be able to take your industry by surprise and yet still be free to walk away from the idea if it begins to look like too risky a hand to play. Just like the poker small suited connector, the business small suited connector gives you the opportunity to win a huge pot by risking only a small one. Let's take it step by step.

Follow Through with Your Ideas

How many times a day do you come up with business ideas? Whether they're giant ideas that you believe could revolutionize your industry or small, seemingly insignificant tweaks or improvements on already existing ideas or products, I'll bet not a day goes by where at least one or two interesting ideas don't come into your head. But something stops you from acting on them. Why? A little voice in your head says things like "I don't have time for that" or "I'll bet there's some reason that idea wouldn't work" or "Somebody else is probably already working on that." What separates the truly successful businesspeople from everyone else is their ability to turn that little voice off and to act on as many of their ideas as possible.

How many times in your life have you come up with an idea only to see it pop up somewhere else a few months or years later? How many times have you thought to yourself, "I had that idea. Why didn't I act on it?" How many times has an opportunity to advance yourself popped up in your office and you've let it pass you by, only to find a colleague taking advantage of that opportunity just a few days later? How many great inventions have you come up with in your head while traveling to work, reading the newspaper, or drinking your coffee, but for one reason or another that little voice in your head convinces you to forget about it? "It's not worth it. It's just a pipe dream." Well, it's about time you told that voice in your head to take a hike. I'm telling you from personal experience, it's the people who are able to ignore that negative voice in their head that are able to take giant leaps in their careers.

The ideas you come up with throughout the day but don't act on are *exactly* the things you need to be acting on. No matter how big, no matter how small, you need to be following through with as many of your ideas as possible. After all, nobody's going to advance your career for you—you're going to have to figure out how to do that yourself. Sure, you could be patient and wait for that status quo raise, but don't you think you're smart enough and talented enough to make that next step in your career *right now?* Taking advantage of these ideas, knowing how to act on them, is how you're going to make that big leap.

But you can't just jump into every idea headfirst. That'd be too big a risk. You don't want to quit your job and dedicate your life to one particular idea or vision only to have it fall apart in your lap. That's the equivalent of going all in with 6-7s before the flop. What happens if the flop doesn't help you at all? Remember, small suited connectors work so well because they're easy to fold if you don't like the look of the flop, just as they're easy to win with if you do like the look of the flop. So how do you take advantage of your ideas without diving headfirst into all of them? By putting all the little pieces together.

Putting the Pieces Together

The way to win big without taking big risks is to get other people involved. By getting as many different people involved in your ideas as possible, you share the risk. The three main risks you avoid by involving more people in your idea are the *financial, temporal,* and *political* risks.

The financial risk is obvious: the more investors involved in getting your idea off the ground, the less personal financial risk you have to take. The temporal risk means that the more people you have involved in your idea, the less time consuming the project will be for you personally. If a new idea takes up too much of your time, it could negatively affect the main areas of your job or any other ideas or projects you are working on. Losing too much time on a given idea can make many ideas too risky to take on, but by involving more people, you reduce the time demands and thus the risk.

The final risk you avoid by getting more people involved in your idea is the political risk. If your boss or someone else at your job were to feel you were putting too much time into a given idea outside of your main area of responsibility it could reflect badly on you. Therefore, the more people you are able to get involved in your idea, the less it looks as though you're helming some large project on the sly. You never want your boss or your company to feel as though you're moonlighting with a second project. By involving more people, it simply looks as though you're testing the waters in new industries without letting it seriously affect your work productivity. If your idea pays off for you or your company, you'll look like the hero who was smart enough to keep an eye out for emerging markets and trends.

There are two steps to getting people involved in your ideas. The first is to always keep an eye out for ways in which other people can help you. When I talk with someone, I think whether I could help them or they could help me with a project or idea I'm working on. Meeting people, finding out what they do, and thinking about how new connections and skills can help bring one of your ideas to fruition is incredibly valuable to both parties.

You may not even realize it, but with every person you meet you're making connections in markets, products, and technologies you never had connections in before. By being aware of all these connections and constantly thinking about how you can best utilize them, you'll be rapidly on your way to getting your key ideas moving in a positive direction. Keep a mental record of each person you meet in the back of your mind, or, even better, write them down or Rolodex their business cards under the field or industry they work in so that the next time you have an idea that needs a connection in that particular field, you'll be able to flip through all of your connections and start making phone calls right away.

You don't even have to be in any sort of power position to get these people involved in your projects. In fact, you'll find that it is the more powerful, important people in the world who are willing to make time for interesting opportunities. It's no joke that this is one of the big secrets to success in business. Good businesspeople are constantly looking for fresh, new ideas and will often give you a moment of their time. Better yet, by combining different people and introducing your connections to each other, you help make a connection for someone else—another great reason for people to want to get involved with your ideas. The great businessmen and -women of the world are always looking for new connections and will be glad to take advantage of the connections you have to offer. You see, you're not the only one out there who is keeping an eye out for people with great connections or skills. Lots of other people are doing it as well.

Bottom line: you don't have to be a big stack to make important business connections. I think that the minute you become aware of all the potential benefits that come about each and every time you meet a new person, you'll find that there's a whole world-wide network of people out there just like you who are always looking to get new people involved in their ideas, or to help you get the right people involved in your ideas.

I keep an eye out for new connections constantly. Whether I'm on an airplane or talking to a waitress at a restaurant, I'm always on the lookout for people who can further one of my many ideas or someone else's. You just never know where or when that person is going to appear who has the right connection you need to turn your little idea into a major success.

In fact, for the most part, everything I've done in my career was jump-started by connections I made in the past. It's amazing to me the places in which these people have popped up in my life. When you start actively looking for these connections in your life, I think you'll be amazed as well at the places and the ways in which they begin to appear.

The first job I ever landed after graduating college was at Bank of America. I got that job by directly calling the CFO of Bank of America and asking him if he could help me get an interview. The reason I was able to call up the CFO of Bank of America and ask for an interview in the first place was that he was the father of a good friend of mine from grade school. A connection made way back in grade school was responsible for the start of my entire career!

Don't get me wrong; the job I was given at Bank of America was by no means an act of charity. I had finished an internship in finance at Merrill Lynch and had just returned from Taiwan, where I had completed a study on the Taiwanese stock market. While it's definitely a nice boost to your career when the CFO of the company can personally secure you an interview, I was the one who had to actually nail the interview and earn the job. Keeping an eye out for connections can be a great way to kick-start new opportunities, but to truly succeed you're going to have be able to back up your connections with action and experience.

The second step in getting people involved in your ideas is to constantly share your ideas with as many people as possible. Not only am I always searching for connections with every person I meet, but I'm sound-boarding as many ideas off of them as possible. By pitching your ideas or offering them up in a colloquial manner—either at the end of a meeting or over a business lunch—you'll often find people will become interested in your ideas and want to get involved without your having to proposition them at all. You can always segue into one of your ideas with a friendly "Hey, that reminds me of a project I've been trying to get off the ground," and wait and see if they take the bait. If they don't seem interested, no big deal. But I think you'll be surprised how many times someone will hear one of your ideas and either want to get involved themselves or know someone who could help further your cause.

If you keep all of your ideas locked inside your head, they have little or no chance of ever amounting to anything real. But if you let them all flow out freely into the universe, I think you'll find that things begin to happen; wheels begin to turn and ideas become action. This is how the small suited connector of the business world works.

Take your ideas that seem small at first, just like the 6-7s seems small preflop, and see if it has a chance at success by utilizing all of your connections and pitching it to everyone within earshot. If your idea takes off—people become involved, your project moves forward, and it seems like it has a chance to succeed—then it's easy to bet big on the idea and take down a big pot. If no one takes the bait and your idea lies stagnant, then it's easy to walk away from it as well. No harm, no foul. By always keeping your fingers in as many pies as possible, you will keep everyone guessing as to what you're going to do next. If you want to take a big leap in your career, you've got to be trying out new ideas all the time. You've got to give yourself every chance possible to succeed by learning to stop second-guessing all of your out-of-the-box ideas.

I'm sure everyone reading this book knows of at least one problem that can be solved or an opportunity that can be taken advantage of. Yet you're not talking about it or doing anything about it. Why? These are exactly the things you need to be acting on. Talk about these ideas with your colleagues and friends. Talking about them is the first step to bringing them to life. These are the ideas that, if they work, can propel you to a whole different level in your career.

The best way I can think to show how you can use small suited connectors in your business life is to show you how I used them in mine. The following are a few examples of the small suited connector in action.

MY EXPERIENCES WITH SMALL SUITED CONNECTORS

A few years back I developed a product called the LapSaver, which I've mentioned before in this book. I think it's a great example of how a good idea can fall apart, and I think it serves as a good parable for what happens to so many businesses. It's also a great way to show how much you can learn from one mistake. The LapSaver project may have fallen apart, but the lessons I learned because of it have made me the businessman I am today. It also happens to be a perfect example of a small suited connector in business.

I was twenty-one years old when I first came up with the idea for the LapSaver. I did a lot of work on the go at that time in my life (and still do actually) and felt as though there was no great product on the market that could serve as a portable table for a laptop. I wanted a product that would keep my laptop steady on my lap, keep the heat from my laptop off of my legs, and yet be portable enough to fit in my laptop case. After doing a little research I realized there was nothing like this on the market, so I took it upon myself to create one.

This was my first entrepreneurial endeavor, and I didn't have any start-up experience. My first step was to build a prototype. I hired someone to build my prototype for a total cost of exactly forty dollars, including parts and labor. With that prototype I set up a business model and prepared my pitch to take out to possible investors. The list of investors I decided to take my product to was put together 100 percent by connections I had made in the years prior to that. I had been working for Bank of America for a few years and knew a handful of wealthy investors. Even at the ripe old age of twenty-one, I already knew to always keep an eye out for beneficial connections in every person I met. The names and connections I had compiled in my few years of business experience were enough to put together quite an impressive list of potential investors.

With my prototype, my business model, and my list of investors, I went out into the world and began pitching my product. In just a short period of time I was able to raise a pretty nice chunk of change. How much, you ask? I raised over $400,000 in investment money. Not bad for a twenty-one year old in 1992. With that money I was able to go into production with my product, take it to market, and even start designing an entire line of products in the vein of the LapSaver. Eventually, the start-up fell apart, partially due to my lack of experience and partially due to the company I partnered with going bankrupt, but it was an incredible experience and probably better than any business master's program I could have attended.

The simple idea of a product that could make a laptop sit more comfortably atop someone's lap is something most people would think about for a few seconds and then come up with some excuse as to why they should forget about it. Yet, it's ideas like these that can lead to huge financial opportunities. Although the LapSaver didn't make it, it turns out that there is a market for products just like the LapSaver in today's economy and I'm sure that if I had been able to keep my company afloat for a while longer I could have made a successful business out of it. I acted on an idea that at first glance seemed outside of my abilities, yet by taking the time to utilize my connections and plan out a business model I was able to put together what was, at the time, a decent start-up company.

From years of making contacts and connections and keeping a mental list of all of these people, I knew just who to go to with my LapSaver idea and found the majority of them very interested and receptive—enough so that I was able to raise a lot of money with nothing more than a prototype and a business plan.

By combining my passion for the idea with my connections, I was able to play my small suited connector and turn it into a mighty big hand. While I lost the hand in the long run, it was still the right play to make. The risk/reward ratio was well in my favor. After all, the only risk I took was in the $40 dollars I spent on the prototype. The reward was $400,000 in capital to put together a start-up business with a lot of potential. I'd bet $40 to win $400,000 with almost any two cards I was dealt at the poker table. I'll bet you would, too.

Of course, not all of my ideas pan out. Some of them lead to great opportunities and some of them don't. But every idea that comes into my head gets its day at the fair. By making new connections every day and sharing my ideas with people I meet, every idea I come up with—no matter how big or small—is given a chance to become something real, to become something exciting. Each of my small suited connectors is a chance at winning a big pot, yet none of them cause me to risk my whole stack.

Even Yahoo! itself, the company I work for today, was in many ways the product of a small suited connector. Yahoo! was started in 1994 by David Filo and Jerry Yang, two students making their way through Stanford's electric engineering doctorate program. They started Yahoo! as a home-brewed collection of their favorite sites on the World Wide Web, originally naming it "Jerry and David's Guide to the World Wide Web." It was purely a way for them to categorize their favorite Internet sites all in one location for easy accessibility, both for the general public and for themselves. They eventually changed the name of the site to Yahoo! and within a year of launching, Dave and Jerry's home-brewed website was getting over a million hits a day. Not bad for 1994—the early days of the Internet.

Yahoo! soon attracted the interest of venture capital groups, especially Sequoia Capital, who, in 1995, gave Yahoo! an initial investment of $2 million. In April of 1996 Yahoo! launched a highly successful IPO (initial public offering) with a total of forty-nine employees. Today Yahoo! is used by more than 375 million individuals per month, is globally the number one Internet brand name, has thousands of employees across the globe, and worldwide reaches the largest audience on the Internet.

Dave and Jerry took a very small risk—operating a homemade website created mainly for their own use and entertainment—and played it to win a huge pot: creating the Internet's most recognized brand name and one of most heavily trafficked sites on the World Wide Web. Not bad for a couple of PhD candidates with a trailer full of computer equipment. Dave and Jerry followed through with an idea they believed in, fueled the endeavor with their passion for the Internet, and stuck by their vision all the way to the end.

The small suited connector is by no means a shortcut. While this great secret of the poker table and the business world has the power to propel you ahead in your career very quickly, you're going to have to put in the work to become an all-around, versatile player. Just knowing how to take advantage of small suited connectors will never be enough on its own to make you a consistently strong competitor. You're going to have to follow all ten rules in this book and work hard at them if you want to become an agile, competitive player in the business world and at the poker table. The small suited connector is a great way to make big leaps from one level of your career to the next, but everything that happens while you're at those levels is going to have to be equally strategic and productive if you're going to survive.

All you need to make a big leap in your career is vision. While this book can't teach you that, most likely if you picked up this book, you already have the self-awareness and the vision needed to know that you could be doing more in your career every day. If this book is going to teach you anything, I hope it teaches you to keep your eye out for all types of opportunities. Just as pocket aces can often be a losing hand, the 6-7s can often be a big winning hand. You've got to stay aware and alert for opportunities, the obvious ones as well as the not so obvious ones.

I've always favored the opportunities that aren't so obvious. I think it's the less obvious opportunities that benefit you more than the obvious "big hand" opportunities, mainly because these "under the radar" ideas keep everyone around you guessing. They keep your colleagues, your bosses, and your industry guessing. Regardless of the size of your chip stack or your position at the table, when you've got everyone around you guessing as to what type of hand you're going to play next, you'll always be poised for success.

THE SHOWDOWN

Play small suited connectors to win the *big* pots,
risk only the *small* ones, and keep everyone
around you guessing. The small suited connector
is one of the great secrets of success in business
and in poker.

KNOW WHEN TO PUT ALL YOUR CHIPS INTO THE POT
Going All In

There are very few strategy games on this planet in which you can put everything on the line at any given moment—in which you are allowed to put every chip you own into the pot and gamble it all on one single play. There are even fewer card games in which, at your whim, you're allowed to gamble all of your money on a single hand of cards and shout out "I'm all in!"

Blackjack, roulette, and craps often allow players to wager as much as they would like on a single hand, a single spin of the wheel, or a single roll of the dice. But in these games of luck you're betting against the house or the casino, not betting against another player.

When you push all your chips in at a Blackjack table, nobody groans, looks down at their cards, and worries that their hand isn't strong enough to win the pot. Nobody is forced to rethink their entire strategy or is put on tilt because you decided to pull all your chips on the line at the craps table. An all-in bet in roulette isn't strategic; in fact, it means nothing more than just what it is—a large bet.

On the other hand, an all-in bet at a No-Limit Hold 'Em game can come on like an atomic bomb. An all-in bet at a No-Limit Hold 'Em game can completely change the course of a friendly home game or rearrange the entire roster of a high-stakes tournament. An all-in bet can knock a big stack down to a small stack, it can turn a favored poker pro into a long-shot, and it can turn an amateur player into the World Series of Poker champion. There is no play in any other game in the world that has as much power as the all-in bet has in No-Limit Hold 'Em.

Very few players can handle the all in. Hell, even some professional poker players out there stay as far away from No-Limit Hold 'Em as possible, unable to handle the psychology of a game that allows one player to put another player to a decision for all of his chips any time he or she pleases. It's the giant swings of No-Limit Hold 'Em that make it such an unpredictable and yet fascinating game. It's the fact that you can go all in with pocket aces just as easily as you can with 2-4 unsuited that makes the game so exciting and so intense. It's also what makes poker so similar to business.

I believe it is this exact ability to go all in that has made the game of No-Limit Hold 'Em so unbelievably popular. I think people have begun to realize how similar the game is to their business life. They've started to see the game, subconsciously or not, as a metaphor for the way in which they interact with their fellow human beings on a day-to-day basis. After all, people don't interact with each other based on numbers or probabilities; they interact with each other based on psychology and strategy. The ability to go all in in No-Limit Hold 'Em is what makes the game more than just a game where "my five-card hand beats your five-card hand"—it makes the game *real*.

Games like chess and Go serve as similar battlegrounds for mental warfare, yet nothing is at stake. Sure, nobody likes to lose in chess—no one likes to have their pride hurt by losing to a superior player—but pride heals. You're not really putting anything on the line in a game of chess or a game of Go—you walk away unscathed whether you win or lose. In No-Limit Hold 'Em, depending on the stakes you're playing for, you could have your entire financial future up for grabs on a single hand. Most people would never play for those kind of stakes (and they'd be right not to), but even if you're playing for pocket change, there is something real up for grabs when you play No-Limit Hold 'Em. There are real-life, tangible stakes, and therefore to go all in—to evaluate whether or not it's worth it to put all of your money on the line—is to take a real, visceral risk. It gets the blood pumping. It's what elevates the game beyond just a simple card game.

In today's crowded global economy you've got to fight tooth-and-nail to carve out a niche for yourself. While taking small risks to win big pots (as covered in rule 9), is the safest and often the most beneficial way to make a big move in your career, you're going to have to take a few huge risks and make a few big moves if you're going to survive for the long haul. No-Limit Hold 'Em is a game that perfectly mirrors that struggle to come out on top; that journey to find one's place in the world. It is in No-Limit Hold 'Em that today's modern businessmen and -women have found a great place to hone their skills, to master their strategies, to practice taking risks and to learn the true measure of their courage.

It's the ability to go all in that makes these things possible, which is why I've saved this topic for the final chapter. Not only is knowing when to go all in the most difficult aspect of the game, I believe it is an utterly essential business skill—and possibly the most important factor in becoming a strong player in today's economy.

Going all in isn't just a poker play, it's a way of living your life. Going all in is about doing everything in your life to the fullest. It's about having conviction in the strength of your hand. It's about having the courage to put everything on the line to achieve your goals, and most importantly, it's about making your life challenging, fun, and exciting each and every day.

In order to become a strong player in either business or poker, you've got to understand the power of the all-in bet. You've got to know when to go all in, *how* to go all in, and *what* to do when someone tries to put you all in. Whether you're an ambitious small stack or a zealous tycoon, this chapter is going to teach you everything you need to know about going all in.

WHAT IS THE IMPORTANCE OF GOING ALL IN?

Whether it's your career or a poker tournament, there is absolutely no way to win either without going all in at least a handful of times. While you may be able to survive for a short while, in order to make it to that final table or last through an entire career, you're eventually going to come to a point where you either have to put all of your chips into the pot or fold a hand you're not ready to fold. To become a great player you're going to have to put yourself out there and take big risks.

Bottom line: if you want to win, you're going to have to go all in. That's why a lot of people don't last very long in the business world. That's why some players never feel comfortable playing No-Limit Hold 'Em. Both can be very intense. If you're going to play, if you're going to be a competitive, agile player, you're going to have to get used to the idea of going all in every once in a while. But that doesn't mean you should ever go all in arbitrarily. There is the right way to go all in, and there is a wrong way to go all in. In this chapter, as contradictory as it may sound, I'm going to show you the safest way to risk it all.

WHAT EXACTLY DOES IT MEAN TO GO ALL IN?

There are many different meanings to going *all in* in business, but in No-Limit Hold 'Em there's only one: it means to put all of your chips into the pot. There are two different all-in scenarios in No-Limit Hold 'Em: the small-stack all in and the big-stack all in. If you're the small stack and you go all in, you'll either double up your chip stack or you'll lose the whole thing. On the other hand, if you're the big stack and you go all in, you'll either win all of someone else's chips or you'll lose as many chips as your opponent wagered. But for the most part, and in most situations, an all-in bet will either win you a whole lot of chips or lose you the majority of chips you had.

In business, there are many ways to go all in, but I have divided them into two main categories which, I believe, every all-in scenario can be placed. The categories are: My Way or the Highway and Betting Big on Yourself. Let's start with My Way or the Highway.

MY WAY OR THE HIGHWAY

Anytime you give someone an ultimatum, you are making a My Way or the Highway all-in bet. If you tell your boss that without a raise you're going to be unable to stay with the company, then you have effectively pushed all of your chips onto the table and said, "My way or the highway." If your boss doesn't give you the raise, you'll have no choice but to quit—you can't go back on your word.

If you've come to a negotiation, named a price, and stated that the price is fixed and nonnegotiable, then you have made a My Way or the Highway all-in bet. You have set the terms for the deal and have sworn to hold fast to them. If the person you're negotiating with believes your price to be too high, then the deal is off and both of you walk away with nothing. My Way or the Highway.

These types of all-in bets are very dangerous, especially if you're bluffing. The My Way or the Highway bet puts everything on the line between you and an opponent. Whether that opponent is a colleague, a client, a boss, or a corporation, when you make a My Way or the Highway all-in bet, you are making an aggressive move against another player, a move that could forever change that business relationship. Most people don't like to be put to ultimatums, so unless you know what you're doing or have solid reasoning behind your bet, the My Way or the Highway all in should never be made carelessly.

BETTING BIG ON YOURSELF

The other type of all-in bet in the business world is the Betting Big on Yourself bet. Anytime you put everything on the line for something you believe in and are not at the same time making an aggressive move against another player, you are Betting Big on Yourself. Leaving your full-time job to head your own start-up company is Betting Big on Yourself. Taking on a huge project within your company, the size of which you've never taken on before, is Betting Big on Yourself. Even putting your nest egg into the stock market is Betting Big on Yourself.

This is the type of bet that can change your life if you win, or get you closer to the final table than you've ever been before. But if you lose, you're going to be in big, big trouble. Luckily, the Betting Big on Yourself bet affects only you personally (your family and/or employees included). It's a much less outwardly aggressive move. In poker every all-in bet is both an aggressive move designed to steal the majority of another player's chips away *and* a move designed to improve your personal position. In business the all-in bet can be an outwardly aggressive move, an inwardly confident one, or a combination of the two.

Now that I've covered the different meanings of all in, it's time to discuss the right way and the wrong way to make such a daring bet.

THE RIGHT WAY AND THE WRONG WAY TO GO ALL IN

With the sudden influx of new players to the game of No-Limit Hold 'Em, the average number of all-in bets per game has probably quadrupled in the past few years. I don't remember seeing half as many all-in bets at an average game when I first learned to play No-Limit Hold 'Em. Whether I'm playing at a friendly home game or a $200 buy-in tournament, it seems like every three or four hands someone is pushing all of their chips to the middle, standing up, and saying "I'm all in" like they were John Wayne announcing himself as the sheriff to everyone in the saloon in an old western movie.

The increase in the number of all-in bets is most likely due to the popularity of No-Limit Hold 'Em on television, where there really is an all-in bet made almost every other hand. The difference is that the No-Limit Hold 'Em games on television are edited down to the most exciting moments, and are therefore not a fair representation of an actual poker game. If you were to be a part of the audience at one of these televised poker matches, the game play wouldn't seem half as fast or nearly as intense as the version they air on TV. But people want their No-Limit Hold 'Em experience to be just as fun as the ones they see on TV, so they go all in like it's going out of style.

Beyond the urge to re-create one's favorite World Series of Poker moments at their weekly poker game, I think people tend to overplay the all in because it's just plain easier than having to think and be strategic. If you push all of your chips in preflop, then you don't have to think about the rest of the hand. You don't have to think about the strategy. You just sit back and watch as the dealer flips the cards and lets you know whether you won the pot or you lost it.

By going all in preflop you're not bothered with those pesky decisions as to how you're going to play your hand on the flop or the turn or the river. By impulsively pushing all of your chips toward the middle, the second you see an A-K in your hand you don't have to burn any brain cells worrying about semibluffing when you've got a straight draw on the flop, or worrying about how to play aces against a possible set (three of a kind). By going all in preflop the game simply becomes a coin toss. It's as if players are playing only to find out how many times A-K will beat pocket sevens or how many times A-Q will get beaten by pocket jacks.

For many, going all in is the easy way out. It's a crutch they use so as not to have to actually learn how to play the game the way it's meant to be played. Hey, if you want to try and win some money purely on the percentages of how many times a particular hand will beat another particular hand, then there are certainly better card games out there with better odds than No-Limit Hold 'Em can offer you. The reason No-Limit Hold 'Em is the Cadillac of poker and one of the greatest strategy games around is that the game goes so much deeper than just the percentages of the cards and the luck of the draw.

No-Limit Hold 'Em is a battle of wills, not a battle of cards. By going all in simply because you're not quite sure the right way to play your hole cards, you're giving up half of your chances at winning the pot. By going all in with your pocket aces you only have one way to win the pot: by beating someone at a showdown. But by playing the hand strategically you could have the weakest hand and *still* end up winning the pot. It's just common sense to play the hand correctly and not leave it all up to luck. Going all in too often is just sloppy, lazy gamesmanship. It is the wrong way to go all in—and it is one of the biggest mistakes people make in No-Limit Hold 'Em.

Another major mistake a lot of players make in No-Limit Hold 'Em is to go all in purely based on their emotions. Just because you want your pocket kings to win the pot, yet some jerk keeps reraising you, doesn't mean you should push him all in just to get back at him. We talked about this in chapter 4: going all in purely because you're frustrated, or mad, or sick of losing usually means you've gone on tilt. The moment you start making decisions at the card table based purely on your emotions is the moment you switch from a thinking player to dead money. Going all in for any reason other than a rational and/or strategic one is a major mistake. For more on how to stop yourself from making an emotional all-in play, take another look at rule 4, "Leave Your Emotions at the Door."

The right way to go all in is to make a carefully calculated decision to put all of your chips into the pot. There is only one reason to go all in at the poker table: to put your opponent to a serious decision. Whether you're looking for your opponent to call or to fold, you're forcing your opponent to make a big decision with a significant chunk of his or her chips when you make an all-in bet. If you're going to put your opponent to such a big decision, you had better have a good reason to do so. A few of these reasons are as follows:

♣ You have the nuts, believe your opponent has a second best hand, and are confident your opponent will call your all-in bet.

♣ You believe very strongly that you have the strongest hand at the table and that your opponent will call your all-in bet with a weaker hand that has little to no chance of improving.

♣ You believe your opponent has a stronger hand than yours, but you are almost positive that by making an all-in bet your opponent will fold his or her stronger hand.

♣ You have a strong hand, yet you believe your opponent is drawing to a hand that can beat yours and you want to make it too expensive for him or her to continue in the hand.

♣ You believe your opponent is bluffing and will fold his or her hand even if it is stronger than yours if you make an all-in bet.

♣ You have a small stack, are losing too many chips each round because of the blinds, and believe you've just been dealt the strongest hand you're most likely to get before you get blinded to death.

Basically, you want to make an all-in bet only if you believe it is the only size bet that's going to bring about the outcome that you want. If you want your opponent to fold and believe you can cause him to do so by raising with an amount less than an all-in bet, then you should raise with less than your total amount of chips. If your opponent ends up calling your bet with a stronger hand than yours, you'll be glad you didn't go all in. You never want to risk it all unless you believe it is the only way to achieve the desired outcome. If you're looking for a call and your all-in bet makes your opponent fold, whereas a slightly smaller bet would have elicited a call, then you have made a mistake by going all in.

Making sure your all-in bet gets you a call when you want a call or gets you a fold when you want a fold comes down to correctly reading your opponent and staying hyperaware of the game at all times. If you're not confident your all-in bet will elicit the desired reaction, then you should not be making an all-in bet. Remember, going all in is risking *everything*. You never want to get into the habit of risking everything on a whim; you want to do it only with the most amount of information backing it up.

In business it works practically the same. You want to make a My Way or the Highway or a Betting Big on Yourself type of bet only if you believe there is no other way to achieve the desired result. To give your boss an ultimatum for purely emotional reasons is a bad play. If you feel you were disrespected or passed up for a promotion, it is never the right move to walk into your boss's office and demand anything with a My Way or the Highway type of declaration.

Making an emotional all-in bet is probably one of the biggest mistakes people make in business. Just as it is a mistake to storm into your boss's office when you're angry and start demanding things *or else*, it is just as bad an idea to rush into a brand new business venture purely because you're excited by its potential. Just as in poker, it's tempting to see those pocket aces and push all of your chips toward the middle knowing you have at least a 50 percent chance at winning the pot. But if you just slowed down and took your time, patiently planned out your business model, or played the aces with a bit more strategy, you'd find that your chances of winning would rise beyond 50 percent. Playing the hand patiently and strategically keeps you in control of the outcome a lot longer than if you were to go all in the moment you were dealt a strong hand.

So when do you go all in in business? When you're as positive as you can be that it is the only way to win. Going all in must always be an extremely carefully calculated move in business. While you should rarely go all in at a No-Limit Hold 'Em table, the amount of times you will probably go all in in your career could be counted on two hands. Going all in in business is a big move. Whether it's a major career change, the helming of new business, or even a big move to save your job, going all in is something you only want to do when you're as sure as possible that you're going to win. Here are a few of the good reasons to go all in in business:

- ♣ You have an extremely strong position within your company and feel the higher-ups would rather give you a promotion or greater responsibility than risk losing you.

- ♣ You have an extremely strong business plan, which you've researched fully and believe to be as strong a business plan as you've ever seen. You also feel this new business concept has greater potential than the job or company you are currently with.

- ♣ You believe a deal or contract that you are negotiating will fail to prove advantageous unless you make an ultimatum or set a strong limitation. You are also fairly positive that the party you're negotiating with will react in the desired manner to your offer.

- ♣ You believe you are in a weak position—either at your job or in a negotiation—and believe that only by making a big all-in type of move will you be able to prevent the job or deal from falling apart.

- ♣ You believe the person you are negotiating with—be it a client, a boss, or a rival company—is bluffing. You believe that by making a bold My Way or the Highway all-in bet you will expose his or her bluff and turn the negotiation around in your favor.

♣ You feel so strongly and/or passionately about taking on a particular business venture or deal that you'd never forgive yourself if you let it slip away—no matter the consequences or the risks involved. This one is tough to recommend, but sometimes you just have to make a Betting Big on Yourself all-in bet in order to respect yourself in the morning.

While I recommend that you be as careful as possible when you go all in, that doesn't mean you should *never* go all in. As I said earlier, in order to succeed in the business world, you're going to *have* to go all in at least a few times in your career. After all, no one is going to make your career a success but you, and in order to make it a success you're going to have to make a few big moves and take a few big risks.

HOW TO GO ALL IN WITH A SMALL STACK

Going all in is done completely differently when you're the big stack in comparison to when you're the small stack. If you're the big stack, going all in is a lot easier. One of the nice things about No-Limit Hold 'Em is that when you're the big stack and you go all in and lose, you only lose as much as your opponent had in his or her stack. For example, if your opponent had only fifty bucks and you had a thousand, even if you went in with your thousand bucks you would only be risking fifty, since that's all your opponent was able to wager. Having the most chips at the table means no one has the power to push *you* all in. When you're the big stack, even if you were to put all of your chips on the line and lose, you would still be in the game. While no one wants to lose a big chunk of their chip stack for no reason, being the big stack means there is a bit more leeway in terms of which hands you can go all in with (considering that it won't be your *final* play of the game). Going all in with a small stack is a completely different story.

Usually, going all in is an *active* play. It's putting everything on the line in an aggressive fashion, devil may care. Going all in with a small stack is a defensive move. When you have a small stack and you know that you're going to lose a good chunk of your chip stack every time the blinds come around, you have no choice but to take a stand and go all in. By going all in with a small stack, you're trying to climb your way out of a hole, double up your stack, and get back on your feet.

The fact is that you have very few options when you're the small stack. You have to act and act quickly. Therefore, you've got to play the first decent hand that comes along. Virtually anything better than a hand in the decent category or any hand with an ace is a good Alamo hand. You've got to decide how strong your hand needs to be in order to give your small stack its best chance of doubling up. This comes down to figuring out how many blinds you can survive before your stack has dwindled to a point where it wouldn't matter if you doubled up or not—it would be too little too late.

In business the equivalent of going all in with a small stack is when you feel you're backed into a corner and have no leverage. The goal of your small stack all in is to regain the footing you need or buy the time necessary, in order to level out your situation so you can begin to rebuild your stack. This happens a lot at the beginning of your career. When you're attempting to build a name for yourself in your company or within your industry, almost every move you make is an all-in move. When creating a table image for yourself at your new job or in your industry, any mistake you make, or any pot you lose, can be a heavy loss to take.

Unfortunately, when you're a small stack, you don't have as

many options as the rest of the players in the game. The best advice for a small stack, either in business or in poker, is to make sure that your hand is as strong as you believe it can be given the amount time you have left in which to act. Whether you're on thin ice with your boss or you're starting your first job, when you're a small stack, you often have a limited amount of time in which to turn things around and/or create a positive image for yourself. Wait too long to make that move and you might have blown your only chance at mending the situation or proving your merit. Play the best hand that you're dealt, take advantage of the best situation possible in which to repair the situation, but don't fold too many decent hands in the hope that a better one will come along.

WHAT TO DO WHEN SOMEONE TRIES TO PUT YOU ALL IN

If another player puts you all in, first and foremost, decide whether or not you think you can win. Whether it's a boss giving *you* an ultimatum or a big stack forcing you into a major decision, the first step in deciding whether or not to call someone else's all-in bet is to figure out your chances of winning the hand. If you aren't very confident that you will come out the victor, then you should fold your hand. If you aren't almost positive that you're going to win the hand, then there's absolutely no reason to be calling someone else's all-in bet. Never fight just for the sake of fighting. Don't let someone else's all-in bet put you on tilt and force you to make an emotional call.

The only time it is easy to go all in is when you have the complete and total nuts and are almost positive that your opponent will call any bet you make. Going all in in any situation outside of that one is going to be a very risky endeavor. They don't call it all in for nothing. Knowing when to go all in is a matter of choosing your battles wisely. You've got to decide for yourself what is important to you in your career and you must be willing to take the necessary risks in order to achieve those goals.

Most people spend their entire lives working in the same industry or doing the same job, which is why you've got to find a way to make that job meaningful. You've got find a way to make that job fun. Going all in means living your life to the fullest by putting your full weight behind each major decision you make in your career. *It's about gambling big to win big.*

Just as in No-Limit Hold 'Em, there is no limit to what you can wager and no limit to what you can risk in your business career. For that same reason, there is no limit to how much you can win or how great your rewards can be. As long as you're willing to make a few big all-in plays a handful of times in your career, you'll find there are no limits to what you can accomplish.

There's no other game like it in the world.

THE SHOWDOWN

To succeed in business you need the courage to go *all in* at least a handful of times in your career. If you go *all in* with wisdom and with patience—at the right time and for the right reasons—you will find there is no limit to what you can achieve.

EPILOGUE

In closing, it is my hope that the theories and information presented in this book prove to be valuable to you in your career. While writing this book, I found that nearly every poker player I spoke to commented on how they often find themselves using their poker skills away from the poker table. Even poker legend Phil Hellmuth told me recently, when I had a chance to meet and speak with him, that he uses poker strategy in his business dealings "all the time." Considering the way Phil's been able to promote himself as a poker player both in his partnerships with online poker sites and in the countless other Phil Hellmuth–branded products, it comes as no surprise that Phil's a poker pro even without two hole cards in his hand.

While few of us have what it takes to be a poker pro like Phil Hellmuth, all of us have what it takes to achieve greater success in our careers. As I said at the beginning of this book, if you've got passion for what you do, a thirst for experience, and a love for making new connections, then seeing your job as a game of No-Limit Hold 'Em should be easy—and it should be beneficial as well. You owe it to yourself to make your job as fun as your weekly poker night. Whether your career needs a major change or just a small tweak, I hope this book inspires you to give yourself the career that you deserve: a career of success and happiness.

On your path to success and happiness I hope you are able to use the lessons you've learned in this book. I hope that you remember to understand yourself, to always be aware of your situation and your surroundings, to keep your eye on your position and your chip stack, to take advantage of a good hand when you're lucky enough to get one, and not to take any loss too hard—even a big loss. You can't expect to win 'em all. Remember, never let a loss dissuade you from taking that next big all-in move. Without the courage to go all in, you'll never win.

Finding great success in your career isn't going to be easy—no easier than winning a major poker tournament—but it is within your power to make it happen. Even your weekly poker night gets tougher week by week as the players learn to adapt to one another and gain a deeper understanding of the game's strategies. The most important thing to take away from this book is that in order to be successful in your career you have to find a way to make your job fun. Life is too short to hate your job day in and day out. Sure, we're all going to have a few bad days, but if you find yourself truly unhappy, it's time to take a critical look at your situation. It may even be time to make a big change.

If you're like most of us, you don't hate your job—you just believe it could be a little better. Well, this is the perfect opportunity for you to start treating your job like a game. It's time to have fun! What can you do to push the table around a bit and start collecting chips? What's it going to take to make more money? Do you have an idea for a new product or a new service that you've been sitting on for a while and just haven't done anything about?

Now is the time to start acting. Now is the time to start playing the game.

I hope that tomorrow, as you walk into your office, you'll be thinking about your chip stack and your next move. Is tomorrow the right day to pitch that new product or make that big move? Is tomorrow the right day to play your hand tightly, or the right day to go all in? Either way, as long as you put the same strategic thinking into your career that you put into your weekly poker night, you will be way ahead of where you were before. Not simply because you'll have a greater chance at achieving success, but because you'll be having a whole lot more fun while you're doing it.

So get back to your job and play hard. Play to win—and go all in!

—Geoff Graber

ACKNOWLEDGMENTS

Geoff: I'd like to thank my family, friends, and colleagues who helped make this book possible. First and foremost: my profound thanks to my good friend David Obst who connected my hand in dramatic style, "runner-runner," after I told him my idea for a book about business and poker. He had much to do with what you hold in your hands today and I doubt it would have happened without him. I would also like to give a big thanks to my agents: Christy Fletcher and Emma Parry and the other fine people at Fletcher & Parry. And I have much appreciation for my publisher Judith Regan, our editor Doug Grad and everyone else at Regan-Books and HarperCollins who contributed to this effort.

I also want to express my gratitude to everyone at Yahoo! who has supported me through this project. It's a long list: first, Pat Ford, my poker coach and friend, who got me hooked on Hold 'Em and inspired this book in many ways. The entire Yahoo! Games team — I wish I could name you all here my friends, colleagues, and poker partners. I've enjoyed working and playing with you! All my friends in corp dev: thanks Toby, Keith, Gerald, Mike, and Damon for all the support, vision, and laughter — let's keep it going. To Sarah Ross, for always caring, encouraging me and thinking of new ways to help Yahoo!. Jo Stevens for getting the world to take notice and for watching out for me. Libby Sartain for showing me the way as a fellow Yahoo! author and helping make Yahoo! a great place to work. The amazing Dan Rosensweig, for his guidance and wisdom. And, finally, to Yahoo!'s incredible founders Jerry Yang and Dave Filo and our wonderful CEO Terry Semel.

Lastly, but most importantly, I want to give a huge thanks to my partner in this book Matt Robinson who did a tremendous job putting my thoughts into words and for being patient when my day job spilled over to our weekend work time, as it almost always didd. Matt is a poker ace, an excellent writer, and an even better person. I could not have found a better coauthor. He has a long and exciting career ahead of him.

There are many others who have inspired me over the years and who drive me to be better. That is my goal, always. I want to thank each of you for being in my life and for your support and caring: my wife Ellen, my parents Peter and Suzanne, my lifelong friends Bruce and Vik. Thank you all.

Matt: David—my mentor, my ally, for thinking of me, for putting Geoff and I together, for making my writing career happen, and for seven hundred other things he did along the way to make this book a reality. Geoff—for the great idea, for the long hours, for the friendship, and for making it fun and easy. My agents: Christy and Emma, and everyone at Fletcher & Parry for always being so helpful and diligent. A huge, huge thanks to Doug Grad our wonderful editor, and to Alison Stoltzfus, Judith, and everyone at ReganBooks and HarperCollins.

To those I love and who helped in countless ways: my mother— Suzanne Budd, Nana, Dad, Cori, Marcy, Janet, my beautiful and perfect Lisa, Barbara and Larry Gerber, Oly Obst, Cara Dellaverson, Jensen Karp, BJ Serviss and everyone from our weekly poker game, Josh Assael, Jamie Hawkins, Dobby Dobertson, Jacob Shapiro, and Eric Kessler—for teaching me the game years ago.